P9-DDS-034

# Missions Now

Tabernacle Presbyterian Church
Indianapolis, Indiana 46205

# Missions Now: This Generation

Roger S. Greenway
John E. Kyle
Donald A. McGavran
with
Timothy S. Penning

With a Foreword by Billy Graham

**BAKER BOOK HOUSE**
Grand Rapids, Michigan 49516

Copyright 1990 by
Baker Book House Compány

Printed in the United States of America

**Library of Congress Cataloging in Publication Data**

Greenway, Roger S.
    Missions now : this generation/Roger S. Greenway . . . [et al.];
  with a foreword by Billy Graham.
       p.    cm.
    Includes bibliographical references.
    ISBN 0-8010-3838-3
    1.  Missions.    I. Title.
BV2061.G72   1990
266—dc20                           90-46639
                                                        CIP

Unless otherwise indicated, all Scripture quotations are taken from the New International Version. Copyright 1984 by the International Bible Society.

# CONTENTS

5

# Foreword

In this book, three veteran missionaries share with today's young adults the vision, motivation, and challenge they feel for world evangelization. Among them the authors represent more than one hundred years of service in missions.

Donald McGavran, at ninety-three, died while this book was in the final stages of production. He was a prolific writer, educator, and mission strategist. Born of missionary parents in India, he spent his missionary career in that country and at the age when most men retire, founded the Institute of Church Growth that later became the School of World Mission at Fuller Seminary.

John Kyle is the director of Mission to the World, the foreign missions arm of the Presbyterian Church in America. He served with the Wycliffe Bible Translators in the Philippines and elsewhere, and as the U.S. Missions Director for InterVarsity Christian Fellowship. His name became well known to thousands of young people during the time he served as the director of the triennial Urbana Conventions.

Roger Greenway served as a missionary to Sri Lanka and Mexico and later as the executive director of World Ministries of the Christian Reformed Church. He taught at Westminster Seminary in Philadelphia and now teaches world missiology at Calvin Seminary in Grand Rapids, Michigan.

The authors' zeal for obeying Christ's commission burns

brightly. Their prayer is that your generation will become more committed to world evangelization than any previous generation in history.

Biblical insight, personal experience, and a broad perception of the vast mosaic of humankind characterize this short book. In every chapter the central goal of missions is clear—to reach every man, woman, and child with the gospel, to multiply churches, and to extend the kingdom of the Lord Jesus.

The greatest need and only lasting hope of the human race is to hear, believe, and follow Jesus Christ. By missions and evangelism the news about Christ is announced to the world. There is no greater challenge than this.

Therefore, I recommend *Missions Now: This Generation* to every young person in whose heart the Spirit of God is placing a call to Christian service. This book will challenge you to go to the tough places in the world, to grapple with the issues that are highest on God's agenda, and to experience the supreme satisfaction of being on the cutting edge of God's plan and purpose in your time.

May yours be the generation that so exalts Christ that it surpasses all others in vision, zeal, and sacrifice for world evangelization!

BILLY GRAHAM

# Introduction

The command of Christ is clear: "Go and make disciples of all nations" (Matt. 28:19).

The prophecy as to what will happen when the command is obeyed and the mission completed is also clear: "This gospel of the kingdom will be preached in the whole world as a testimony to all nations, and then the end will come" (Matt. 24:14).

The resources needed to carry out Christ's orders are available:

- 5 million evangelical churches worldwide that acknowledge Christ as Savior and Lord and adhere to his Word, the Bible
- Billions of dollars in disposable income in the hands of committed Christians worldwide—all the money necessary to support the missionary enterprise
- 100 million evangelical young people worldwide (if even a fraction of one percent will obey Christ's command and commit themselves to the evangelization of unbelievers, this generation can change the world)

The divine power required for the task is abundantly supplied: "All authority in heaven and on earth has been given to me" (Matt. 28:18); "you will receive power when the Holy Spirit comes on you; and you will be my witnesses" (Acts 1:8).

The need of the hour is that we obediently submit to God's will in missions, seeing the world as he sees it and responding to its needs as he leads.

At the beginning of the twentieth century, a missionary statesman by the name of John R. Mott traveled all across North America speaking to students about missions. Through him thousands of young people heard Christ's call and responded obediently. Mott recognized that "to generate real missionary enthusiasm an educational campaign is needed. It is impossible to create zeal for an object on which people are ignorant. The basis of all healthy enthusiasm is truth and sincerity. The zeal that endures and grows and achieves is according to knowledge."[1]

As we near the beginning of the twenty-first century, the three of us wrote this book because we believe Christian missions is still the world's most important and exciting enterprise. Each generation is responsible before God to reach men and women with Christ's message of salvation and love.

Read this book prayerfully, with your will submitted to Christ's Spirit. The needs throughout the world are enormous. Half of the world's population is under twenty-one years of age, and most of them do not know Christ as Savior and Lord. That's your challenge. They are the ones you must reach.

J. Oswald Sanders has said: "The responsibility of evangelizing this vast throng lies squarely on the shoulders of the Christian youth of this generation." It's *your* generation he is talking about.

Yours is the generation now called to evangelize and multiply churches in the megacities of Asia, Africa, and Latin America; to translate God's Word into the hundreds of dialects whose speakers still have no portion of Scripture; to reach the unreached tribes, castes, neighborhoods, and other segments of mankind; to reevangelize the once-Christian West where secularism and materialism have emptied churches, leaving behind a remnant of believers. The spiritual and material resources you need for these tasks are available; all you need to do is use them.

As the three of us have listened to the Word, examined the world, and responded to the Lord's call in *our* generation, we place the missionary challenge before you. We are confident of your faith and commitment to serving Christ, and we believe that through you Christ will honor his name throughout the earth during the vital years of your own generation.

The authors are grateful for the editorial assistance provided by Timothy S. Penning and the secretarial service of Nelvina Ilbrink in the preparation of this book.

# PART 1

## GOD'S PLAN
## AND
## WORLD MISSIONS
## TODAY

# 1

# THE MODERN WORLD
# AND GOD'S WILL

## Donald A. McGavran

Television, air travel, and instant communication have brought about an increasing consciousness that the multitudinous peoples of the world now constitute one vast humanity. This humanity is enormously complex. It is, as we shall see later, composed of at least one hundred thousand segments, or to use the word in the Greek New Testament, *ethnē*. More than three hundred thousand students from practically every country in the world now study in American colleges and universities for a few years before returning to their own lands. Intercontinental students are becoming increasingly common. Students from Africa flood into France, England, Germany, and other lands. Japanese and Filipino students go to Europe as well as to America. The world is indeed becoming one.

The media have made us more aware of places like Namibia on the southwest coast of Africa, Nepal on the northern border of India, Korea in east Asia, and the high country fringing the western border of South America.

These places have become part of the television that we all watch every night.

While the world is becoming one, there are vast differences in its various countries. In some lands 90 percent of the people are illiterate, while in other lands 98 percent are literate. In some lands $300 a year is an excellent income; elsewhere less than $10,000 a year is considered poverty. Some lands have little political and military power, but nations such as the Soviet Union and the United States are formidable powers. Although the world population is complex, we are nevertheless a global community.

Physical hunger, spiritual hunger, illiteracy, overpopulation, endemic poverty, and great riches are persistent aspects of this community. They are all present to some extent in every nation. Every piece of the vast human mosaic, every *ethnos*, is different. Its incorporation in a peaceful, brotherly world is a difficult task. Yet its incorporation is God's will.

Christians therefore ask themselves what they must do in this kind of a world to carry out God's plan for humanity. How can we help multitudes of his children in each of these nations—many of whom have no knowledge of him at all—become disciples of the Lord Jesus Christ, accept the Bible as his revelation, and be filled with the Holy Spirit? Only when multitudes of men and women in every nation believe on Christ and become practicing Christians —sharing the gospel with others—is God's purpose for the world going to be fulfilled.

Sharing the gospel, however, is not easy. There are many concepts of God and the world: Hinduism in India; Buddhism in China and Thailand; Confucianism in China; Shintoism and Buddhism in Japan; Islam in North Africa, Arabia, Iran, Iraq, Pakistan, Bangladesh, and Indonesia; Marxism in the Soviet Union; Roman Catholicism, Lutheranism, Presbyterianism, and Episcopalianism in Europe; scores of branches of the Protestant and Roman Catholic Churches in North America; and Roman Catholicism and Protestantism in Latin America. Animism underlies the dominant religions in many parts of the world.

A tidal wave of secularism has swept across both Europe and North America and among the highly educated in other parts of the world. Peter Brierley, in his publication *LandMARC* a couple years ago, published the following statement:

> The population of England, Scotland, and Wales is 54.5 million souls. Of these, 6 million are regular practicing Christians, 5 million are nominal Christians, 25.5 million are notional Christians, and 18 million are openly atheists, agnostics, secularists, Hindus, or Muslims.

By "notional Christians" Brierley meant those Englishmen who if asked, "Are you a Christian?" would reply, "Yes, I suppose so. I am an Englishman." In other words, 11 percent of the English are practicing Christians; 56 percent are nominals or notionals; 33 percent are non-Christians.

When I was in Finland ten years ago, I asked a leading Christian authority how many Finns were Christians.

"Oh," he replied, "94 percent are Lutherans."

"How many are in church on Sunday?" I asked.

"Well," he replied, "less than 5 percent."

"And on communion Sunday?"

"Less than one percent," he replied sadly.

Three years ago, twenty-four German Lutheran pastors visited the School of World Mission and the U.S. Center for World Mission in Pasadena. After giving an address, I was having lunch with them. I turned to the Lutheran pastor sitting next to me and said to him, "Tell me about your parish, my friend."

He replied, "In my parish there are four thousand people."

"Wonderful!" I exclaimed. "Four thousand souls!"

"Wait a minute," he replied. "Only 100 of these are in church on Sunday, and I have contact with 300 more. But with 3,600 (90 percent of the parish population) I have no contact at all."

Unfortunately, this is increasingly true of community after community in the so-called Christian world. I conducted a survey of a typical American city of 30,000 inhabitants. There were 62 churches, but only 6,000 worshipers could be found in them on an average Sunday. Some of the 24,000 not in church were nominal Christians, but many were either secularists or never attended church at all. In the thousands of rural and urban settings in America the percent of population in church would, of course, vary from this illustration.

It is possible upon reading the figures for the number of Christians in any country—and these facts are readily available—to conclude that the United States is a fairly Christian country. A careful review of the facts, however, makes such an opinion quite impossible. The United States and Canada are countries in which secularism has really swept across the land. The *practicing* Christians in these two countries represent 15 to 20 percent of the population; 70 to 85 percent of the population in North America is composed of either open secularists or heavily secularized "Christians."

The African-American community in the United States (about 13 percent of the population) called itself Christian 30 years ago. Today, however, a large number of African-Americans have become openly secular. Meanwhile, Islam is taking advantage of the intense feeling that the black community as a whole, emerging from slavery 120 years ago, has not been fairly treated by the white "Christian" majority. Islam has won many African-American converts. Ironically, the practice of capturing and selling slaves was only done by Muslims. Muslims in Africa—mostly south and west of the Sahara—attacked villages and marched the strongest men, women, and children two to four hundred miles to the coast where they were sold to the captains of slave ships. Islam has done very little to further brotherhood in the world today.

The New Age movement has become increasingly popular in America today. It proclaims that all religions, including secularism and Marxism, are the ideas of good men. Each should go forward without attempting to convert anyone to its own brand of thinking. The only rational decision today is to allow all men to form their own religious systems and to declare that all religions are ways to the top of the mountain. Whether one takes path 1 or path 21 makes no difference. They all lead upward.

What position must Christians take today, facing this world of many religions and this America so heavily secularized and invaded by the New Age movement? Are all religions equally true? Has the one God, our heavenly Father, created all of them? Or are they merely the convictions of people seeking to describe the world in which they live? Do all religions lead upward? Is Jesus of Nazareth merely one of many men with a vision?

Christians must answer all these questions with an emphatic "No."

An all-wise, all-loving, and all-powerful God created man in his own image. God gave humankind the freedom to believe what was reasonable and true. God did this in order that man may truly be a child of God, to some extent bound by physical laws but nevertheless free to think and plan as he thought best.

Rejoicing in the discoveries of science, however, humankind concluded and believed that this wonderful world—with its vegetable, animal, and human mosaic—was created by a series of atomic accidents. Anthropoid apes, by sheer chance, happened to give birth to a male ape who was five times as intelligent as his father and mother, walked on two feet, and—wonder of wonders—fathered children like himself. Atomic accidents, in a word, became the new god worshiped by secularists. However, God the Father Almighty, maker of heaven and earth, did in fact create the physical world, the vegetable world, the animal world, and people. What has happened is not due to a series of atomic accidents. It was planned by an all-wise and all-powerful God.

God—through Abraham, Moses, Samuel, David, Isaiah, Jeremiah, and others—laid before the twelve tribes of Israel his plan for their lives in revelations and words that the people could understand.

However, the polytheistic societies surrounding the Hebrews conquered them, taught them, served them, and ruled over them. The Hebrew tribes, therefore, frequently departed from God's teachings. They began worshiping the gods of the land—Baal, Astoreth, Dagon, and others.

After the united kingdom of Saul, David, and Solomon had crumbled, Jeroboam of the northern kingdom made two golden calves and placed them at strategic sites. He did not want his subjects going to Jerusalem to worship Jehovah (1 Kings 12:28). Many similar turnings away from God are recorded in the historical books of the Old Testament.

What happened nearly three thousand years ago to the Hebrews is happening again as Christians find themselves in a world where travel and instant communication make what others worship immediately apparent. One hundred years ago, Christians in America saw few houses of worship except Christian churches. Today they see Muslim mosques, Hindu temples, and Marxist meetinghouses. They read books written and published by convinced atheists. They select governors and members of Congress who are thoroughgoing secularists. Non-Christian faiths of many sorts have invaded the United States.

In the fullness of time (year 1 in our chronology) God sent his Son, whose life, teaching, sacrificial death, and resurrection are revealed so clearly in the New Testament. He planted his church, which is the body of Christ. Since the resurrection of the Lord Jesus and the filling of his true followers with the Holy Spirit, the church has been expanding under Christ's direction into every continent and every nation. The twenty-first century may see a tremendous expansion of the Christian faith.

The global population is projected to reach 10 billion in fifty years. The problems facing men and women in this more densely populated globe will be enormous. God has plans which must be discerned. His commands must be obeyed. He does not wish for untold famine. He does not wish for the tremendous killing of men and women, boys and girls. He does not wish for multitudes wandering in an intellectual desert to come up with religions of their own devising. He does not wish for humans to live in the midst of an intellectual fog. He has shown us the right road to follow. We are being led by the Lord Jesus Christ, who proclaims, "I am the way and the truth and the life. No one comes to the Father except through me" (John 14:6). We are also led by God's utterly truthful Word, the Bible.

People who love and follow God's commands are people who have seen the vision of God's intention for his world. It is a vision of God's kingdom, a world of justice and kindliness, of brotherhood and peace. Our vision consists of what the Bible talks about when it speaks of the "kingdom of God." It's a vision of a world in which "God's will is done on earth as it is in heaven." It's a world in which justice is done, kindliness is a common way of life, brotherhood is established, and peace prevails. It is in pursuit of that vision that we rush out to evangelize, multiply churches, and attack all the barriers that sin has erected against that vision and its fulfillment.

All Christians in the 1990s and thereafter must carry on effective evangelism, the multiplication of truly Christian congregations in every piece of the vast human mosaic. That is why a new effective surge of missionary activity must and will occur. That is why every hundred practicing Christians should send out one of their number to be a propagator of the gospel, a multiplier of congregations at home and abroad.

The following chapters will describe some of the main elements of a truly Christian outlook on the world today. As convictions of the sort described in this book are shared with practicing Christians all across America and all other countries of the world, we shall construct the theological, sociological, anthropological, and organizational frameworks thinking Christians need today, if they are to obey God the Father Almighty. The new world order which is in God's clear plan for humanity is what we must envision, work at, pray for, and with God's blessing, bring into being.

# 2

# GOD'S PLAN OF MISSIONS
# ... AND YOUR PLACE IN IT

## Roger S. Greenway

The best advice I can offer to a young Christian is this: *Find out God's plan in your day, and fit yourself into that plan.* Nothing is more fruitful or satisfying than knowing God's plan and coming to terms with it.

The Bible teaches that God had a megaplan for the world from the beginning, and that this plan called for the reconciliation of a fallen and sinful world. To carry out this plan, God conducted a series of missions, or "sendings" ("mission" means sending), involving the three Persons of the Godhead and Christ's body on earth, the church.

The Bible makes clear God's purpose in sending the church on its mission. The church was to proclaim the gospel so it might grow among all peoples. The outstanding mark of the church would be faith in Christ. By faith members of the church would be reconciled to God, and would live in a relation of love and reconciliation to one another. Their reconciliation would be the sign that God's plan for the world was in operation.

The Father's sending of the Son to be the Savior of his people (Matt. 1:21) is at the center of God's mission to the world. By his saving work, Jesus became the head of a new community called the church, a spiritual family belonging to God (1 Pet. 2:4–5, 9–10). Just as Jesus was sent into the world by the Father, Jesus commissioned his disciples. He sent them out into the world in a way that resembled his own mission. "As the Father has sent me," Jesus said, "I am sending you" (John 20:21).

Note carefully the sequence of sendings. God's Son was the primary, divine missionary who was sent by the Father into the world to become the Savior and Lord of his people. The Son sent his disciples, making them missionaries of the gospel and empowering them for their task with the Holy Spirit. Similarly, God sent the Holy Spirit as a missionary Spirit, to bear witness to Christ and to convict the world of sin, righteousness, and judgment (John 14:26; 15:26–27; 16:7–8).

The implications of all this are highly significant to missions. Christ calls his followers to be co-missioners with him. As he was sent and bore witness to the truth about God, so should we. As the Spirit testifies to the truth about Jesus, so should we. In the power of the Holy Spirit we become co-participants in God's great plan, the evangelization of the world and the building of the family of God.

This means that all work done by Jesus' followers in pursuit of their calling is really a part of God's own plan of missions. In missions we are called not only to work for God, but to work *with* God in a manner resembling the sacrificial obedience of his Son, Jesus Christ. This is the glory of the missionary vocation. It is to be co-missioners with Christ.

I use the term "co-missioner" to refer to the believer in Christ who receives from God the threefold task of co-laboring, co-suffering, and co-witnessing with God and fellow believers. By "co-missioning," I refer to the work itself. The Bible expresses the key elements of this work as follows:

- *Co-Laboring*: "For we are God's fellow workers; you are God's building. . .,. As God's fellow workers we urge you not to receive God's grace in vain" (1 Cor. 3:9; 2 Cor. 6:1).
- *Co-Suffering*: "Now I rejoice in what was suffered for you, and I fill up in my flesh what is still lacking in regard to Christ's afflictions, for the sake of his body, which is the church. I have become its servant by the commission God gave me to present to you the word of God in its fullness" (Col. 1:24–25).
- *Co-Witnessing*: "When the Counselor comes, whom I will send to you from the Father, the Spirit of truth who goes out from the Father, he will testify about me. And you also must testify, for you have been with me from the beginning" (John 15:26–27).

These verses portray mission work as a cooperative effort involving believers and the triune God. Believers are called to co-labor, co-suffer, and co-witness in the carrying out of God's global plan of missions.[1]

Individually and successively, the Father, Son, and Holy Spirit share with believers in this work. With the Father, missioners build a living temple of believing men and women. With the Son, the vicarious Lamb, missioners offer their ministry for the reconciliation of sinners. With the Spirit, missioners bear witness to the truth about God and the work of salvation that Christ accomplished.

This is an awesome picture of the imperfect efforts of believers incorporated into the perfect working of God in building his church and gathering his people. These verses teach that God so designed his plan for the world that the plan cannot be completed without the participation of believers in the work of missions.

## Co-Laboring

In the plan of God, the gospel needs a voice. The good news cannot announce itself. It must have a human announcer. John the Baptist said, "I am the voice" (John

1:23). Note carefully: not merely a sound or noise, but an intelligent, articulate, human voice was required to point the world to Jesus. This has been true in every age.

The Bible teaches that God employs missionaries as his ambassadors: "We are therefore Christ's ambassadors, as though God were making his appeal through us" (2 Cor. 5:20). Ambassadors are official representatives. They are sent to a foreign land on behalf of the government that appoints them. By virtue of their appointment, ambassadors have authority. Theirs is the authority of the state that commissioned them. As ambassadors, they do not deliver their own messages but the messages given them by the government they represent.

The governments ambassadors represent speak in their words and act through their acts. The government stands behind them with all its power and authority. Anything said or done to ambassadors is regarded as being said or done to the government that commissioned them.

The same can be said of the ambassadors of Christ who speak God's truth and carry out the instructions their Lord gave them. Insofar as they faithfully deliver God's Word, God speaks in and through them. Behind them stands divine power and authority. This chain of ambassadorial authority and representation is linked to the order of sending, as Jesus indicates: "Whoever accepts anyone I send accepts me; and whoever accepts me accepts the one who sent me" (John 13:20).

In 1 Corinthians 3:9, Paul states, "For we are God's fellow workers; you are God's field, God's building." A more plain statement of co-missioning could hardly be found. In both construction work and agriculture, there are various roles and functions, and there are different workers. Some workers are highly skilled, while other workers have lesser ability. Workers don't all do the same thing, yet each contributes to the total endeavor.

God, the divine Architect, is building a spiritual temple composed of believers in his Son, Jesus Christ. God builds according to a plan of his own design. Among the workers he employs, some are master builders while others are common laborers. Some labor at an early stage in the program, while others are enlisted in the final stages. Some have menial tasks, whereas others seem to have glamorous assignments. But when someday the building stands completed, each worker will be able to point to some part of the plan and say, "I was the worker in that time and place. That was my part in the construction. That's where God used me."

Paul says, "I planted the seed, Apollos watered it, but God made it grow. So neither he who plants nor he who waters is anything, but only God, who makes things grow. The man who plants and the man who waters have one purpose, and each will be rewarded according to his own labor" (1 Cor. 3:6–8).

Each faithful worker must carry out a given assignment in the overall plan and operation. The soil must be tilled, the seed planted, the ground cultivated, and the harvest brought in. The underlying assumption is that God works his farm through his servants and that their faithful labor is indispensable if success is to be achieved in the total operation.

Observe the balance: all the workers' labor would yield no crop if God did not send sunshine and rain. Yet, regardless of the soil's fertility and the provision of sunshine and rain, there would be no crop without the labor of the workers in the fields.

In God's plan of missions, the efforts of divine and human "co-workers" result in God's harvest being brought in. Certainly, it is one of the mysteries of God's wisdom that in the building of his house and the harvesting of his fields, the outcome of his sovereign plan depends on your labor and mine.

## Co-Suffering

Not long ago, a fourteen-year-old girl in central China was one of a group of nine young evangelists who were arrested by communist cadres for preaching the gospel.

They were beaten and forced to kneel continually all day and night. The third day, the girl fainted and the authorities released her. The others continued to kneel in prison for eight nights and nine days.

When the entire group was eventually released and the girl was reunited with them, she began to cry. "Why are you crying?" she was asked. "You should be happy because your friends have been released." She replied, "They suffered for Christ for nine days, and I suffered for only three days."[2]

Persecution and suffering are increasingly the experience of Christians in many parts of the world. From the martyrs of Uganda to the imprisoned and tortured evangelists in China, to the Christians who are attacked and discriminated against in India and Muslim countries, the list grows longer and the degree of suffering more intense. Worse things may lie ahead, and Christians must get ready by understanding suffering in the light of Scripture and the price of gospel proclamation.

Paul's language in Colossians 1:24 is startling: "Now I rejoice in what was suffered for you, and I fill up in my flesh what is still lacking in regard to Christ's afflictions, for the sake of his body, which is the church." Is Paul suggesting that Christ's suffering was not complete? Could there be some quota of suffering "still lacking" that we must meet?

The explanation begins with the acknowledgment that Christ's vicarious suffering for our redemption was completed once and for all at Calvary. At the same time we recognize that God's redemptive work as a whole advances to completeness by successive stages. When the Savior exclaimed on the cross, "It is finished," it was his atoning death that was complete. When he rose from the dead, his justifying work was complete (Rom. 4:25). When he sent the Holy Spirit, the applying agency was completely supplied.

But one more step had to be taken. The cross, the empty

tomb, and the poured-out Spirit needed a proclaiming voice to tell of Christ who died for sinners and rose for their justification. Mouths were needed to be channels of the inspiring Spirit. And the mouthing of the gospel would entail suffering and sacrifice.[3]

Arthur T. Pierson, one of the great spokesmen for missions in the nineteenth century, spoke of the "four links" of the chain of reconciliation between lost sinners and a holy God. There was the link supplied by the cross, that replaced the broken link of the law. There was the link the resurrection supplied, replacing the broken link of a righteous life. The Holy Spirit supplied the broken link of love. Each of these three links was essential, yet one link was still missing.

The fourth link may surprise you. Paul speaks of it in Romans 10:14–15, where he raises the question of how people are to hear the gospel of Christ and be saved unless someone tells them, unless the church sends preachers, and unless heralds of the good news go forth. The answer is obvious. Lips anointed by the Spirit and speaking the message of Christ are the fourth link in the chain of reconciliation. Lips are an indispensable link. The story of the cross and the empty tomb must be told. The unction of the Holy Spirit must fall upon lips of obedient servants if God's plan for sinners' redemption is to be completed.[4]

Yet co-missioning can be costly. What sufferings should obedient servants of the gospel expect? Paul answers that question from his own experience. In 2 Corinthians 11:23–33, he lists the hardships he has endured for the sake of his mission. He was imprisoned, beaten, stoned, shipwrecked, exposed to constant danger, worn thin by overwork and deprivation, and constantly felt the pressure of concern for the churches with their needs.

Paul obviously knew what was meant by Christ's "afflictions, for the sake of his body, which is the church" (Col. 1:24). For that reason he never let young Christians harbor the idea that Christian discipleship would be free of suffering. The entire New Testament witnesses that early Christians regarded suffering for Christ as inevitable (see 1 Pet. 4:12). The benefits of suffering were extolled (Rom. 5:3–4), and a godly life free of suffering was considered an exception (2 Tim. 3:12).

When Jesus trained the disciples he forthrightly declared that they should expect suffering in the course of serving him. In Matthew 10, which describes the missionary "internship" of the twelve disciples, Jesus spoke clearly about the kinds of suffering and opposition that the disciples were to expect. Some people would welcome them and receive their words. But others would reject them, hate them because they came from Jesus, and persecute them severely.

"A student," said Jesus, "is not above his teacher, nor a servant above his master. It is enough for the student to be like his teacher, and the servant like his master. If the head of the house has been called Beelzebub, how much more the members of his household!" (Matt. 10:24–25).

Jesus himself made it plain that there was a cross for each disciple to bear, and that co-suffering, losing one's life for Christ's sake, would remain a guiding principle of Christian service and discipleship (Matt. 10:38–39).

### Co-Witnessing

Christ explicitly and repeatedly promised the Holy Spirit as his witness, the empowerer of the disciples, and the illuminator of truth. Christ spoke of him as the "Spirit of truth" who would guide believers into all the truth, and as the one who would "bring glory to me by taking from what is mine and making it known to you" (John 16:14).

The special office of the Spirit is that of bearing witness to Christ. He does not speak of himself, testify to himself, or glorify himself. His mission is to put Christ's person, saving work, and glory into prominence. The Spirit testified to Christ before the incarnation by inspiring the Old Testament prophets and writers who foretold Christ's coming. The Spirit testified to Christ when he came by empowering his words and works, and by inspiring the

Evangelists to record accurately the story of Christ's ministry and teaching.

The Spirit continues to testify as he applies the word of the gospel, causing each new believer to see and believe that Jesus is Savior and Lord. The Spirit likewise testifies through believers as he uses their lives and lips to spread the news of Jesus. "You also must testify," said Jesus to the disciples (John 15:27). After Pentecost, Peter and the other apostles confidently declared, "We are witnesses of these things, and so is the Holy Spirit, whom God has given to those who obey him" (Acts 5:32).

In what sense can we speak of believers co-witnessing with the Spirit? There was, first of all, the special witness of the early apostles who had been with Christ during his earthly ministry and could testify firsthand to his words and works, as well as to his death and resurrection.

But what of the co-witnessing in which all believers share, throughout the centuries and still today? How important is their witness?

First of all, believers convey an external witness through words and actions that reach the eyes and ears of those who are brought into contact with the gospel. The Spirit cooperates in the believers' witness in the sense that he motivates and empowers their testimony.

But more than that, the Spirit produces an internal witness in the recesses of the mind and heart. This is far beyond anything believers can do alone. The witness of believers is necessary, but it can never go beyond the eyes and ears of the physical body. Only the Spirit can speak with a voice that carries all the way to the soul and heart.

Still something more must be added. For there is a sense in which believers can bear witness to the great truths of salvation in ways which the Spirit of God cannot duplicate or replace. When believers in Christ witness to God's saving grace, they do so as redeemed sinners. From experience they bear witness to God's love in Christ that makes all things new.

In God's plan of missions, believers are the Spirit's

instruments, his co-witnesses, in the application of Christ's work and the transformation of sinners into saints.

Andrew was instrumental in reaching Peter. Philip was used to reach Nathaniel. The Ethiopian on the desert road was taught the gospel by Philip. Saul heard the message preached by Stephen. Peter became the Spirit's channel to reach Cornelius. Paul and Silas communicated the gospel to the Philippian jailor.

The history of missions after the close of the canon is consistent with the earlier pattern: the Spirit uses believers to communicate God's saving message. So far as we know, there are no exceptions. In all his ordinary workings, the Spirit employs human co-witnesses in the divine activity of applying Christ's saving work to human hearts and lives. Throughout history, every person converted to Christ was witnessed to in some way by a Spirit-led believer.

In a small town in southwestern Brazil, I baptized a man who gave a remarkable testimony on the day of his baptism. He came with a tattered old Bible that he had read over and over for thirty years.

He said that when he was a young cowboy out on the range, he did a great deal of reading. From a certain novel he learned about a book called the Bible. He began to pray that if such a book existed, God would send him a copy. He inquired around town, but nobody had a Bible or knew where to obtain one.

One day he was riding his horse near the only highway in that part of Brazil. As a bus went by, he saw a passenger throw something out of the window. When the bus had gone, he rode over to the object lying on the ground. It was a Bible. God had answered his prayer. If the person on the bus didn't want it, this cowboy certainly did. From that moment he never doubted that this Book was a gift from heaven.

Who threw the Bible out the window? Nobody knew. Nor did anyone know the circumstances leading up to the event. Yet the Spirit of God had been working ahead of time arranging that a cowboy who had prayed for a Bible would be waiting along the road to pick it up.

Strange as it may seem, that is how the Spirit often works when believers co-witness with him to Christ's word and grace. The form of their witness, such as giving a Bible, provides opportunity for the Spirit to carry out his saving operation—often with surprises.

How exciting to know that because of God, even the small things we do to point others to Jesus may have eternal results! That's the excitement shared by all those who purposefully fit their lives into God's plan of missions.

# 3

# WHAT IS GOD DOING?

## Roger S. Greenway

In the introduction to his challenging book, *The Great Omission*, Robertson McQuilkin describes an incident that took place at an Urbana missionary conference several years ago.[1]

Speaking to a group of students on the subject of world evangelism, he made the point that more than half the world's people not only had never heard the gospel of Jesus Christ, but were out of range of witnessing churches. Despite this, pitifully few Christians were attempting to reach them.

Unexpectedly, a voice rang out from the back of the auditorium: "How come? How come so many are unreached, yet so few are going?"

"That is a very good question," replied McQuilkin. "In fact, I know Someone who asks that question every day."

"Who's that?" queried the student.

McQuilkin gestured toward heaven, and a hush fell over the audience.

How come?

That question has haunted McQuilkin ever since.

He offers five reasons why missions suffers:

1. We don't care that much.
2. We don't see very well.
3. We think there must be some other way.
4. Our prayer is peripheral.
5. Someone isn't listening.

It's a good list—accurate and to the point. Missions suffers because lukewarm Christians don't much care about the things Christ cares about supremely.

Missions suffers when Christians are ignorant of the needs of the world, and don't see the millions who are unsaved, unchurched, and uncared for.

Missions suffers when church members assume that if God wants the unevangelized peoples of the world brought to him, he'll do it somehow. They sense no need to pray about it or to get personally involved.

Missions suffers when the subject is not preached and taught from Scripture, and the church doesn't hear the heart-throbbing call to go forth and evangelize all nations and peoples.

But take heart, for there is exciting news!

The exciting thing about the world today is that in many places renewal in missions is occurring as fresh winds of the Spirit blow across the world. This renewal is widespread and well documented, and any Christian or denomination that is not experiencing it should be jarred into asking why not.

David B. Barrett, editor of the *World Christian Encyclopedia*, is the foremost researcher of church growth and current trends in missions. In a recently published article, "The Twentieth Century Pentecostal/Charismatic Renewal in the Holy Spirit, with Its Goal of World Evangelization," Barrett writes about the growth and renewal of Christian groups.

A "third wave" of spiritually renewed Christians is sweeping across the world. These new Christians represent the growing churches of Asia, Africa, and Latin America as well as Western denominations. They are not to be confused with the classical pentecostals, who first appeared at the beginning of this century, or the Protestant and Roman Catholic charismatics of the 1960s and 1970s.

Third-wave believers are members of mainline or independent churches. They exercise the gifts of the Holy Spirit without identifying themselves as either pentecostal or charismatic in the traditional sense. They stand at the forefront of the present-day advance of the gospel.

The challenges they face are not hard to identify. Large segments of the earth's population are controlled by communist or Muslim governments, both of which are hostile to Christian missions. Yet even in places of intense opposition and persecution, Barrett notes that charismatic growth is explosive and uncontrollable; the sheer magnitude and diversity of the numbers involved are incredible.

As we sense the excitement in all of this, it is important to remember that the source of missionary revival is the Spirit of God.

The Spirit who creates in God's people a fresh interest in missions, gives them eyes to see a lost and hurting world, and drives home to them the message that they are responsible to obey Christ's commission in their generation, is none other than the missionary Spirit of God.

The Spirit yearns to see lost sheep found and wayward children converted and brought home. Whenever you see that same yearning in the minds and hearts of believers, you know the Spirit of God is at work.

In many traditional churches and long-established denominations, there are believers who hunger for missionary revival. They hear what is happening elsewhere and they sincerely desire to be part of God's moving in the world.

Where should they begin? How can they be sure that what they desire to be part of is indeed the plan of God? What can be done to motivate churches to become part of this renewal in missions?

The clue to the answer, I think, lies in going back to the Bible and rediscovering what it says about world evangelization. When we hear what the Scriptures say, our ears are tuned in to the missionary spirit of God.

In the preface to his book, *The Mission of God*, George F. Vicedom makes this same point: "We shall never achieve any missionary results from our theology and church work unless we allow Holy Scripture to give us the necessary missionary impetus. Only when we have grasped the fact that the whole purpose of the Bible is the rescue of mankind and therefore mission work, only then do theological thought and every type of church work receive their proper direction."[2]

Let's try to clarify the central idea of missions as it is found in the words of Jesus. Shortly before his ascension to heaven, Jesus Christ gave his disciples a missionary mandate which we call the "Great Commission." The words are recorded at the end of each of the four Gospels and at the beginning of the Acts of the Apostles.

Each account of the mandate is unique and essential. Each represents a fragment of something Jesus said on a separate occasion. For our purposes I will put the expressions together and highlight the key ideas.[3]

> Jesus came and stood among them and said, *"Peace be with you!"* After he said this, he showed them his hands and side. The disciples were overjoyed when they saw the Lord.
>
> Again Jesus said, "Peace be with you! *As the Father has sent me, I am sending you."* And with that he breathed on them and said, "Receive the Holy Spirit." (John 20:19–22)

> Then Jesus came to them and said, *"All authority in heaven and on earth has been given to me.* Therefore go and make disciples of all nations, baptizing them in the name of the Father and of the Son and of the Holy Spirit, and teaching them to obey everything I have commanded you. And surely *I am with you always,* to the very end of the age." (Matt. 28:18–20)

Then he opened their minds so that they could understand the Scriptures. He told them, "This is what is written: The Christ will suffer and rise from the dead on the third day, and *repentance and forgiveness of sins will be preached in his name to all nations,* beginning at Jerusalem. *You are witnesses of these things.* I am going to send you what my Father has promised; but stay in the city *until you have been clothed with power from on high.*" (Luke 24:45–49)

He said to them, *"Go into all the world and preach the good news to all creation.* Whoever believes and is baptized will be saved, but whoever does not believe will be condemned. And these signs will accompany those who believe: In my name they will drive out demons; they will speak in new tongues; they will pick up snakes with their hands; and when they drink deadly poison, it will not hurt them at all; they will place their hands on sick people, and they will get well."

After the Lord Jesus had spoken to them, he was taken up into heaven and he sat at the right hand of God. *Then the disciples went out and preached everywhere, and the Lord worked with them and confirmed his word by the signs that accompanied it.* (Mark 16:15–16, 19–20)

On one occasion, while he was eating with them, he gave them this command: "Do not leave Jerusalem, but wait for the gift my Father promised, which you have heard me speak about. For John baptized with water, but in a few days you will be baptized with the Holy Spirit.

You will receive power when the Holy Spirit comes on you; and you will be my witnesses in Jerusalem, and in all Judea and Samaria, and to the ends of the earth." (Acts 1:4–5, 8)

These separate expressions of the Lord's final mandate offer the following key ideas about missions:

- A double salutation of peace to those whom the Lord sends (John 21:19, 21)
- A declaration of divine authority (Matt. 28:18)

- An outline of the essential truths of the gospel, Christ's atoning death and resurrection, and repentance and forgiveness of sins, based on Old Testament Scriptures (Luke 24:45–47)
- A clear expression of the mandate to be witnesses, to preach and make disciples (Matt. 28:19; Mark 16:15; Acts 1:8)
- An indication of the universal scope of the mandate (Matt. 28:19; Mark 16:15)
- A declaration as to the source of power by which to carry out the commission (Luke 24:49; Acts 1:8)
- An assurance of the Lord's personal presence, and of signs accompanying those who believe (Matt. 28:20; Mark 16:17–19)
- A summary of the fulfillment begun, as the disciples obeyed their ascended and exalted Lord's instructions (Mark 16:19–20)

Volumes have been written about each one of the key ideas in the Great Commission passages. Central to them all is the concept of witness. The word is found in two of the key statements of the Great Commission (Luke 24; Acts 1), and is probably the word that best summarizes the will of Christ for his church throughout the world.

The New Testament is filled with witness terminology and illustrations. Sometimes witness means the person who tells what he or she knows about Christ. At other times it means the testimony the person gives. In other places it appears as a verb, meaning to bear witness, to utter a testimony for the Lord.

The witness is a person who knows and tells essential information about Jesus Christ—who Jesus is and what Jesus has done for the reconciliation of people who, because of sin, were alienated from God and from other people.

Any individual who knows the Lord personally can bear witness. Even a child can be a witness. Witnesses know that they are sinners and that Jesus saves from sin, and testify to the saving grace of Christ that gives life and forgiveness, and makes everything new.

The content of the witness is always Christ and the gospel. The witness points to Christ, the Light of the world and the Savior of mankind. The purpose of the witness is to give glory to God and to draw people to him in the fellowship of the church.

Christ himself is heaven's supreme witness. The witness of believers is possible and effective because Christ's Spirit endows their words and actions with divine power.

Here lies the missionary apostolate today. Witnessing to the living Christ links the church in every era with the fellowship of the apostles and their mission. This simple command to fill the world with the saving knowledge of Christ is the duty and privilege of all believers. All who are saved are to bear witness, and all who are unsaved are to hear the testimony. In that great endeavor the labors of the apostles continue.

To enter into apostolic work means to accept personal responsibility for the lost in this generation. Wherever that truth is understood and applied, missionary revival and church growth invariably occur. Where it is ignored or rejected, churches stagnate and witness dies.

Unfortunately, misconceptions about the matter have crippled many churches. "Being a good Christian," to many people, means simply accepting the Bible, professing to be a follower of Christ, attending church services, giving offerings, being honest and charitable, and living in a decent manner. But personal responsibility for witnessing to a lost world? That idea hardly enters the picture as far as most Christians are concerned. They consider missions to be the private concern of a fringe group of enthusiasts.

Jesus, on the other hand, gave the missionary mandate to all who follow him. Responsibility for worldwide witness is part and parcel with being Christ's disciple. Any view of discipleship that has no place for personal responsibility toward the lost is as flawed as a view of salvation that leaves out faith.

The only discipleship the Bible knows is an apostolate of faith and practice, of confession and proclamation, of the knowledge of salvation and personal witnessing to the saving Lord. Nobody can have Christ and shrug off a lost world.

Many of us at times may wish that Christ had assigned the missionary task to angels instead of to us. I am sure the angels would have accepted the challenge gladly and begun heralding the good news everywhere.

But there was something that angels could not do, and that is why the task was given to Christ's disciples and not to angels.

Angels could have become great *preachers* of the gospel, but they could not be its *witnesses*. Witnesses are men and women who themselves have experienced God's saving grace in Christ. They bear testimony to the fact that Christ has lifted them personally out of sin and condemnation and set their feet on the road of righteousness, peace, and joy.

Angels, not having sinned and not having tasted personally the grace of salvation, cannot tell the good news in the way you and I can. Only redeemed sinners can be personal witnesses to Christ's redeeming work. That is why the missionary mandate is every true believer's highest privilege and continual responsibility.

There are indications that the Spirit of God is awakening the church to realize that the missionary mandate is for all disciples everywhere. The reason the church is in the world is to bear witness in the power of the Holy Spirit to Christ and salvation.

In many parts of the world, new mission agencies are being formed. These agencies are offering missionary training, and missionaries are being recruited who represent a new wave of spiritually renewed Christians reaching out in bold witness for Christ. They are crossing old barriers of language and culture, often suffering persecution in order to present the gospel to followers of other faiths and ideologies.

This makes the present era a very exciting time for

Christians. The revitalizing winds of the Spirit are blowing across the world, bringing fresh zeal for obeying Christ's Great Commission. Even skeptical observers must admit that this is an era of renewal in missions.

It is sometimes said that the Acts of the Apostles is the only "unfinished book" in the Bible. As you read the last chapter, it appears as though the story is incomplete.

At the beginning of Acts it says, "In my former book . . . I wrote about all that Jesus began to do and to teach until the day he was taken up to heaven." The words "former," "began," and "until" imply that something had been going on before in the gospel narrative; in Acts the writer intends to give the "latter" part of the story. Acts will tell all that Jesus continued to do and teach by the Holy Spirit after he was taken up to heaven.

Yet when we examine the last chapter of Acts, it strikes us that the story trails off unfinished. We are told that Paul stayed in Rome in his own rented house, welcoming all who came to him, boldly preaching the kingdom of God and teaching about the Lord Jesus Christ. Then the story abruptly stops.

Is that the proper way to end such a narrative? No other book in the New Testament concludes that way.

The reason is that Acts is the "book of a witnessing church." And that book will not end until the witness is also concluded. The story will go on as long as the Spirit who empowered the early disciples continues to carry Christians forward and outward in obedience to the Great Commission.

The simple truth is that the story of Acts will not end until all the peoples of the earth have been evangelized, the last witness spoken, and the last testimony to God's grace in Christ believed or rejected. To be a part of that story is every believer's privilege and responsibility. Today, the Spirit of God is stirring the church in a way unmatched since the days of the apostles.

What a shame it would be, not to be part of what God is doing at this time.

# 4

# THE CHALLENGE
# TO YOUTH TODAY

## John E. Kyle

Your generation will reach the prime of life in the twenty-first century. That makes you a very special group of Christian people. The world in which you live and serve the Lord Jesus will be an entirely different world than the world of the previous century. The opportunities ahead of you are enormous.

Christian youth who are firmly committed to Jesus Christ as Savior and Lord will be directly responsible for reaching their generation of lost people. This principle of young Christians reaching their own generation must be followed until the return of Jesus Christ. That is why world missions presents a particular challenge to you on the eve of a new millennium.

Today you have information concerning world missions that can be readily understood—a privilege that few previous generations have enjoyed. Literature on missions has been written with you in mind. World mission conventions, such as the Urbana Student Missions Conventions for North America and the Missions Congresses for

Europe, have been planned with you in mind. Thus, you have opportunities to become informed and to grow in your knowledge of a world made up of billions of people who do not know Jesus Christ as Savior. In his book, *On the Crest of the Wave*,[1] Peter Wagner states there is a "fourth world" that consists of people located in any place, at any time, who do not know Jesus Christ as their Savior. These people are the target groups about whom you need to be informed in order to act intelligently in reaching them with the gospel.

Jesus Christ, when here on earth, continuously challenged those who were seeking to follow him. When Zacchaeus climbed a tree to get a better view of Jesus, he suddenly heard Jesus declare to him: "Zacchaeus, come down immediately. I must stay at your house today" (Luke 19:5). Jesus also challenged the woman at the well when he said: "Will you give me a drink?" (John 4:7). Today Jesus Christ is in the business of challenging young people to a deeper commitment.

The challenge is to have a consistent walk with Jesus Christ in the midst of a society that offers a host of activities and monetary enticements to lure you away from being a fruitful disciple. John Stam, who was martyred in China in the 1930s, said while he was studying at Moody Bible Institute the most difficult area of his life to maintain was not his studies or Christian service but his hour-a-day quiet time. However, his classmates and friends attested to his Christ-like lifestyle.

Growing Christians would be expected to be keen witnesses through sharing their faith in the Lord Jesus Christ. However, I've learned through interviews with young people who desire to enter career missionary service that they have not had a fruitful evangelistic lifestyle. I encourage you, therefore, to learn how to share your faith in Christ in two ways: (1) by learning a meaningful gospel presentation; and (2) by consistently sharing a relationship to Jesus Christ with others.

Only God himself produces belief in others through the

work of the Holy Spirit, but he sees fit to use Christians as channels of information to share the gospel while they are on earth. Start sharing your faith and see how God uses you!

You are more enlightened about world conditions than any generation that has ever lived on earth. More than thirty thousand young people have the opportunity each year to serve abroad in short-term missionary assignments. You can test your readiness to bear witness to Christ cross-culturally by going overseas or by reaching out to persons of other cultures here at home.

An enlightened worldview will enable you to carry out the multiplying factor of missions—discipleship. It is important that you not only lead people to Jesus Christ, but also guide them into a deeper relationship with him. As you lead people to Christ they will, in turn, lead others to Christ.

In order to grow as Christians and prepare for the challenge you need to seek out other young people for weekly fellowship in small Bible study groups. Bible study and a daily quiet time will prepare you to share how God is at work in your life.

You must become involved in a vibrant local church that manifests evangelistic fervor coupled with a profound searching and teaching of the Scriptures. By doing this you will grow as a Christian in a life-changing fellowship with others who are growing in Christ. You should find a mature Christian to whom you are accountable for your Christian growth and conduct. If someday you go overseas to serve as a missionary or become a leader in a local church here in North America, you will discover there is little place for "lone rangers" in Christian ministry.

It is also important that you become familiar with the biblical basis for world missions. You need to understand that it is not man's own desire to reach others for Christ in other cultures, but that it is God's desire that the lost be saved. This fact from God's own heart is taught repeatedly from Genesis to Revelation, illustrating that a concern for the lost is heavy on God's heart. God's burden is actually the purpose for our local churches. Churches are to reach out with the gospel in the neighborhood, city, state, and nation, to the uttermost parts of the world.

Become conversant with and knowledgeable about the biblical stalwarts such as Moses, David, Gideon, John, and Paul. Learn about men and women God has used mightily in contemporary times. Amy Carmichael, Jim Elliott, Hudson Taylor, Mary Slessor, William Borden, William Carey, William Cameron Townsend, and a host of others have made a great impact for Jesus Christ on the world. Reading their biographies will challenge you and encourage a belief that the Lord can use you, too, in your lifetime to make a difference in the course of the world's history.

God is looking for youth who are wholeheartedly committed to Jesus Christ, who have counted the cost to be different, and who are willing to go anywhere and do anything to make the gospel of Jesus Christ real and alive. Mission-sending agencies in the United States are looking intently for such youth to fill a multitude of important and crucial missionary positions overseas.

Ultimately, you must come to grips with the fact that your living pattern can change the course of the world. If you live your life for the glory of Jesus Christ, you can actually change history. When William Cameron Townsend went to Guatemala to sell Spanish Bibles, he was only a teenager, but he had a heart for God and lived his life for the glory of God. As the co-founder of Wycliffe Bible Translators while still a young man, Townsend put into motion a movement for God that has since sent more than six thousand missionaries all around the world. They have translated the Scriptures into hundreds of languages. They have changed the lives of individuals, tribes, and groups that came under the influence of the Word of God, had their sins forgiven, and were given a new life and a fresh hope. We do not often realize what one life can do to change the course of history.

There are many opportunities to get involved in missions. As the "Cambridge Seven" stayed on in Great Britain to recruit other missionaries after graduating from college in 1885, young college graduates today have formed groups called Caleb Teams. Their sole purpose is to recruit other young people to join those already committed as missionaries to go overseas with them as career missionaries. The Caleb Project has two teams which visit college and university campuses as well as local churches in a recruiting program. Various mission-sending agencies, such as Wycliffe Bible Translators and Frontiers, Inc., assign some of their young missionary candidates to such teams for up to two years of itinerant service. Their challenge is: "Come along and join us in overseas missionary service!"

The Urbana Student Missions Conventions are held every three years at the University of Illinois campus in Champaign-Urbana, Illinois, in late December. These conventions are planned specifically with young adults in mind. The sessions are targeted to an audience of college-age young people, young working adults, and high school seniors. The purpose of the convention is to help young people focus on world missions from various points of view. There is challenge, motivation, and education for each participant, with an opportunity to become committed to the cause of world missions. In the past, such plenary speakers as Billy Graham, Luis Palau, Helen Roseveare, and Tony Campolo have challenged young people to become involved in world missions. More than 150 overseas mission-sending agencies are present to share their overseas ministries with the delegates. Some 18,700 young people attended Urbana '87.

College students have been organizing other mission conferences as well, inviting others to attend and become interested in world missions. In any one year more than three thousand young people attending these conferences are exposed to the cause of world missions. They hear outstanding mission speakers, attend workshops on various mission subjects, and interact with career missionaries who are present to counsel the young people. Many missionaries have been recruited through these college and university conferences across North America.

In the midst of a generation made up of materialistic "yuppies," you are faced with the dramatic challenge of adopting a different lifestyle. Much has been said about the benefits of a simple lifestyle, but little has been done in the Christian community to carry out such a concept. Your generation should consider a more realizable, moderate lifestyle that will allow faster repayment of educational debts. Then, finances would be freed up to invest in the cause of world missions. This is not a call to a radical lifestyle, but to a manner of living that would stand as a witness to others who are bent upon a quest for materialism, for "me, myself, and I."

It is my belief that you are extremely well equipped because of your youth, and you possess the adventurous spirit that is needed to step out boldly for Jesus Christ in the area of world evangelization. While young, you can accomplish great things by faith in Christ. You need to utilize and develop your individual gifts so that you can join with others in reaching the lost of your generation for Jesus Christ.

# PART 2

## THE CHURCH
## AND WORLD MISSIONS

# 5

# YOUTH IN ACTION

## John E. Kyle

Often we are led to believe that elderly ladies are the only prayer warriors standing behind missionaries sharing the gospel on the front lines. We thank God for the older Christians who pray vigorously for the cause of world missions. But the news needs to get out that there is an increasing number of young adults entering into the ministry of intercession on behalf of missionaries serving overseas.

At the Urbana '87 Student Missions Convention, 10,000 copies of Patrick Johnstone's *Operation World* were sold in 20 minutes to young adults leaving the assembly hall following a plenary session. This 270-page book has been a prayer guide to thousands of young adults during the past decade as mission agencies such as Operation Mobilization promote its use around the world. At the same convention more than 5,000 copies of David Bryant's *Concerts of Prayer* were sold. This book tells believers how to pray in groups for revival of individual Christians, churches, and communities linked with a concern for world missions.

Young people are involved in the promotion of times of

concerted prayer on college and university campuses across North America. In such concerts of prayer people spend two to three hours praying together. This prayer movement has been carried by young people from campuses to local civic centers, encouraging hundreds of small groups of Christians to enter into prayer together.

A growing number of young people are adding to their prayers the financial support of world missions. At Urbana '87, young people gave offerings totaling over $360,000 for overseas mission projects. *World Christian* magazine, as well as the publications of mission agencies, openly share investment opportunities. Adults are often amazed by the amount of funds that Christian young people have at hand to spend for Christian overseas ministries.

Jesus Christ taught a great deal about the importance of investing your money, as well as your whole life, in the building of God's kingdom. In Matthew 6, Jesus emphasizes the importance of proper investment:

Do not store up for yourselves treasures on earth, where moth and rust destroy, and where thieves break in and steal. But store up for yourselves treasures in heaven, where moth and rust do not destroy, and where thieves do not break in and steal. For where your treasure is, there your heart will be also. (vv. 19–21)

When a young man asked Jesus what he had to do to gain eternal life (Matt. 19), Jesus gave him a lesson in investment:

"Why do you ask me about what is good?" Jesus replied. "There is only One who is good. If you want to enter life, obey the commandments."

"Which ones?" the man inquired. Jesus replied, "Do not murder, do not commit adultery, do not steal, do not give false testimony, honor your father and mother, and love your neighbor as yourself."

"All these I have kept," the young man said. "What do I still lack?"

Jesus answered, "If you want to be perfect, go, sell your

possessions and give to the poor, and you will have treasure in heaven. Then come, follow me."
     When the young man heard this, he went away sad, because he had great wealth. (vv. 17–22)

Most young people do not have great wealth, but the finances they do have should be invested in the Lord's work. Churches as well as campus ministries have been hesitant to teach the biblical standards of tithing, with the result that the cause of world missions has been neglected. In 1985, North American Christians for the first time gave more than $1 billion to the cause of world missions. We rejoice in this new record, yet it is a mere pittance to a cause that is so much on God's heart!

William Borden divested himself of his great inheritance before he left for China to serve as a missionary. He died in Cairo, Egypt, at the age of twenty-five. Found written in the flyleaf of his Bible were the words, "No reserves, no retreat, no regrets." Your generation, as good stewards of God's gifts, should be generous with your monetary resources in order to be strategically involved in world missions.

Those concerned for world missions should join together in small groups to share, study, pray, and encourage one another. As some of you prepare to go overseas as short-term or career missionaries, you can grow in your relationship to Christ as you pray for funding, give financially, and provide overall backing for missions through prayer. You may stay in the local fellowship or go overseas. World missions needs both goers and senders, and it is encouraging for missionaries to know that a group is standing behind them as they serve overseas. These small groups are often called "support groups." They share prayer letters from missionaries, invite missionaries to their group to speak, share books on missions, and in general, grow together in their commitment to world missions.

It is also important to study world missions. Mission courses are offered by Christian colleges and seminaries, and a few are available by correspondence. The U.S. Center for World Missions, headquartered in Pasadena, California, offers a special mission course called "Perspectives." The course is presented each year in various cities across the United States and is taught by highly qualified mission specialists.

There are hundreds of books available that can broaden your understanding of world missions. (Twenty-five years ago the selection was extremely limited.) InterVarsity Missions offers an excellent bibliography for those interested in a reading program.[1] The William Carey Library of Pasadena, California, as well as most Christian bookstores carry books on missions for sale. There are excellent videos available on subjects such as "Being a World Christian" and "Concerts of Prayer" that can be used both as study materials for small groups and in local churches.[2]

Studying world missions from a book or tape, however, is not the same as "hands-on" involvement. Nothing is more exciting or instructive than sharing Jesus Christ and discipling new Christians. To facilitate this experience, programs of short-term missionary service sprang up in the early 1960s. In 1965, 540 Christians were involved in short-term overseas programs ranging in length from a couple of weeks to two years. By 1973 there were 3,500 such short-term missionaries; and in 1985 there were 27,933! These numbers were reported by mission-sending agencies such as Wycliffe Bible Translators and Africa Inland Mission; no count was taken of the large numbers sent out directly from local churches in North America.

By 1989 there were close to 60,000 short-term missionaries serving overseas from North America. By comparison, the total number of evangelical Protestants serving overseas as career missionaries from North America numbered around 39,000.

It is important to have the right attitude toward short-term service overseas. It ought not to be regarded as a grand tour or a glamorous vacation. Short-term service is serious business for the Lord and a possible gateway to a career in missions.

Short-term missionaries should have the backing of their local church or college fellowship and in some sense should be "selected" by their peers or by an adult such as a pastor. Most short-term experiences are done in a team setting, so that the participant does not have to function alone. It is wise for each short termer to receive some cross-cultural training before leaving North America to ease the shock of living and working in a different culture. Of great importance also are service and responsibility in the local church along with a desire to be helpful to others.

The opportunities for short-term service are many and varied. Participants may be involved in evangelism, construction projects, and other useful activities that assist career missionaries and national Christians. The key for the short-term missionary is to go as a servant and to be willing to do whatever is requested. For service-minded young people there are hundreds of opportunities.[3]

In a short-term mission program you can get the feel of what it is like to serve the Lord overseas. You can "test the waters" to see if you fit into such a ministry as a career missionary. You can better determine the kind of training you need in order to prepare for career service later on. As you prepare for career service, many mission agencies stand ready to assist you by means of counseling.

Short-term service overseas will widen your horizons and enable you to better represent the needs of missions to your fellow Christians at home, inspiring them to become more involved. Former short-term missionaries can pray more specifically for the needs overseas, and they can challenge others to contribute financially to the cause of world missions. Experience overseas can also equip us for effective ministry among students from other nations who are studying in North America's colleges and universities.[4]

As a young Christian adult, you need to prayerfully consider the depth of your involvement in the cause of world missions. There may be legitimate reasons why you cannot go overseas to serve. But you can be a "sender" through prayer, financial support, and other ways. But face the question squarely: What keeps you from applying for career service as an overseas missionary and using your training and spiritual gifts in a cross-cultural setting? It was John Stam, martyred in China in 1934, who as a young adult was greatly influenced by the question: "There are those who cannot go and those who are free to go. Why should both stay at home for the same work?"

# 6

# THE MOSAIC OF MANKIND

## Donald A. McGavran

Some years ago when I was visiting Mexico City, I walked by the university library. On its wall I saw a picture about a block long. I began to wonder how this picture withstood the blazing sun and the slashing rain and the cold and the wind without fading. I drew closer and looked at the picture again. It was not a painting but was made of hundreds of thousands of tiny cubes of glass. Some were black, some were white, some were red, some were yellow, some were pink, some were purple, some were grey. The wind and the weather, the sun and the rain, had no effect on this glass at all. That picture will be there for thousands of years.

Like that picture on the library wall, mankind is a mosaic made up of hundreds of thousands of pieces. There are many different kinds of people, many different languages, many different colors of skin, and many different occupations. The multitudinous minorities in American cities and the variety of castes in India and tribes in Africa and other lands are all evidence of the mosaic of mankind. All Christians must see the task of world evangelization as Christianizing every piece of this vast human mosaic.

The differences among people in the mosaic are not all

physical or racial. The people may be rich or poor, those
who read well or those who cannot read at all, those who
live in dirty rooms in the inner city or those who live in
spacious mansions in the suburbs. Some people are earnest
Christians while others are followers of the religion called
secularism, believing that there is no god.

The mosaic of mankind is continually recognized in the
world by laws, customs, scales of pay, places of residence,
and goals that people set for themselves and their children.
We, as Christians, must determine our God-given role in
this mosaic.

The Bible itself speaks of the mosaic of mankind. In the
Old Testament we read about the Moabites, Ammonites,
Hivites, Jebusites, Philistines, Syrians, and Babylonians.
When the Old Testament tells us about God's people, the
children of Israel, it tells us about twelve distinct tribes.
Once one piece of the Hebrew mosaic—the Benjaminites
—fought all the other pieces of the mosaic. Eventually two
tribes formed the southern kingdom, and ten tribes formed
the northern kingdom. The two tribes of the southern kingdom remained more or less true to Jehovah; the ten northern tribes abandoned the worship of Jehovah, made two
golden calves, and started to worship them.

In the New Testament the emphasis on people groups
continues. While the New Testament makes no mention of
the Roman Empire, again and again we read the word *ethnos* or *ethnē*. This Greek word is defined by the great biblical scholar Gerhard Kittel as a group of like individuals. A
swarm of bees is an *ethnos*; so is a herd of cattle; so is every
tribe, every caste, every clan, every separate segment of
mankind—in short, every piece of the vast human mosaic.

The New Testament speaks about *ta ethnē* frequently.
These words are quite commonly translated as "the
Gentiles." This is because in the beginning all those who
became followers of the Lord were Jews. The big question
was whether the gospel was for the many other pieces of
the human mosaic as well. At first the answer was no. Jews

considered themselves the people of God and felt that only they were to be saved.

But then—believing that God had commanded them to do this—Peter and other Christian leaders baptized Samaritans, an Ethiopian eunuch, a Roman centurion and his household, and Greeks in the city of Antioch. The conviction grew that Christ's command to disciple *panta ta ethnē* (Matt. 28:19) meant discipling all the peoples: tribes, clans, castes, races, pieces of the human mosaic were to be won to Christ.

The Roman world was full of peoples. There were the Macedonians and the Athenians. There were the Galatians. There were the Romans. There were the peoples in Spain, to whom Paul intended to preach the gospel.

We read in the seventh chapter of Revelation that at the end, gathered before the throne in heaven, there will be men and women from every tribe and tongue and people and nation. In short, all the pieces of the mosaic of mankind are clearly recognized by both the Old and the New Testament. Clearly, the mosaic of mankind is a biblical concept.

Now the Bible also says quite clearly that in Christ there is no Jew, no Greek. But it also says no slave, no free; no male, no female. Yet the New Testament again and again says that slaves are to obey their masters, and slavery as an institution is nowhere denounced in the New Testament. It continued as a way of life until the nineteenth century. Even today in a world which proclaims that all nations and people are equal, we have a vast array of tribes and castes and clans, the rich and the poor, the powerful and the very weak.

Equality, brotherhood, treating all men fairly, counting all as equally children of God and therefore brothers and sisters is the goal. By God's grace and Christ's intervention that goal will be reached in the future. But today it is only projected in a very unequal mosaic of mankind. The goal gives us something to work toward. We will reach it at the end of a long pilgrimage. But at present, we live in a world made up of many, many pieces.

The seventh chapter of Revelation tells us that while Christians everywhere should certainly work for brotherhood, peace, and justice, they do this in a world in which there are many, many segments of society. The mosaic of mankind is the reality that we all face, in the midst of which we must carry out Christ's command to disciple all the pieces of the mosaic.

Accepting the reality that mankind is a mosaic of people groups, we must respond to God's command that every piece of the vast human mosaic be discipled. This is emphasized in Romans 16:25–26, where we read that eternal God has commanded—not requested, not suggested, not recommended, but *commanded*—that the gospel, the good news that God grants eternal life to all who believe in Jesus Christ, be proclaimed to all peoples (*panta ta ethnē*). These Greek words, so strange to most Americans, are important ones. In many Bibles they are translated as "nations." In A.D. 1600, when the King James Version was first printed, "nation" frequently meant tribe, clan, or caste. Today, however, "nation" means a political entity such as the Soviet Union, the United States, India, or China. The New Testament, however, never speaks of the Roman Empire, but of *ta ethnē*, the clans, the tribes, the segments of society which made up the one great nation, the Roman Empire. As the gospel is proclaimed, the passage goes on to say, these *ethnē* will be led to faith and obedience. Not every person in each piece will become a Christian, but certainly a large number, possibly even a majority will (Rom. 16:25).

John 3:16 is also relevant: "For God so loved the world that he gave his one and only Son, that whoever believes in him shall not perish but have eternal life." "Shall not perish." If they do not believe, they will perish. But if they do believe, they will be granted everlasting life. This is as true of the most advanced pieces of the mosaic as of the most retarded. It is true in Europe, North America, China, India,

Africa, Latin America, and the islands of the sea. This is the world in which we live.

Thinking men and women must either believe this or believe that we live in a world where a series of atomic accidents has in some super, marvelous way created men of many different colors and many different languages and that these same atomic accidents will one day lead to the desolation and destruction of these people.

Another passage which speaks very clearly and commandingly to the situation is 1 Corinthians 9:1–11:1. To paraphrase this in today's language, Paul asks the question, "When a Christian is invited out to a meal by a non-Christian friend and served meat, should he ask his host, 'By the way, has this meat been offered to idols? If so, I cannot eat it.'"

No, says Paul. The Christian should simply eat it. He does not know it has been offered to idols.

Of course, if he is told that the meat has been offered to idols, then he should courteously decline to eat it. But since most times he will not be told that it has been offered to idols, he will simply eat it. Paul sums up his teaching in two verses, one in chapter 9 and one in chapter 10. In these verses he says, "I have become all things to all men so that by all possible means I might save some." He goes on in 11:1 to a definite command: "Follow my example." Remember that these words are not spoken to pastors, preachers, apostles, deacons, or elders. Rather, they are spoken to all the Christians in Corinth, whether they are laborers or intellectuals, city treasurers or clerks. They are commanded to be all things to all men in order to win some.

The epistles of Paul clearly indicate that one of the chief duties of all Christians is to seek to win their comrades, their relatives, their friends, their business associates to ardent faith in Jesus Christ. If they believe on Jesus Christ, they will not perish; if they do not believe, they certainly will perish.

The third biblical passage to which we will turn is

Matthew 28:18–19. Here the Lord Jesus Christ, speaking to his followers, says to them, "All authority in heaven and on earth has been given to me." Christ uses this awesome authority to say, "Therefore, *matheteusate panta ta ethnē*." The word *matheteusate* means "enroll in my school," or, in Christian terms, "incorporate in my body, the church." *Panta ta ethnē* means all the segments of society—tribes, castes, clans, minorities, neighborhoods. Whether these live in cities or villages, in valleys, on high mountains, on fertile plains, in deserts, or on islands of the sea makes no difference. "Enroll them all in my body, the church." Every piece of the vast human mosaic must be discipled, must be enrolled in Christ's school, must be incorporated in his body, the church. That is what the mosaic of mankind means to practicing Christians today. That is what this command of the Ultimate Authority in the universe has always meant and will always mean to Christians. Tell all mosaics of the Savior, lead them to believe on the Savior, and welcome them into the church, which is the body of Jesus Christ.

What does the mosaic of mankind mean for practicing Christians today? What does it mean for the young men and women who are dedicated Christians? What does it mean for all those who intend to obey the Lord Jesus and to walk in his ways and to learn his Word and to live lives filled with the Holy Spirit?

First, we must recognize immediately the exact nature of the task set before us. Christians lead good lives. They fight for justice, equality, brotherhood, and peace. But before and as they do that, they are to devote their thinking, their praying, their activities, and their goals to proclaiming the gospel and discipling piece after piece of the vast human mosaic. That is the task of all real Christians.

This means that laypersons should make proclaiming the gospel, persuading men and women to believe, and even multiplying congregations their own task. What is commanded by the eternal God, what is commanded by him to whom all authority in heaven and earth has been given, was commanded by Paul in an inspired passage and is certainly a Christian duty. Not to do it is a sin.

Just as men are commanded not to commit adultery, not to rob, not to murder, so they are commanded to disciple all the pieces of the vast human mosaic. This is God's command. All Christians should be carrying it out. To be sure, not all Christians will be missionaries in foreign lands. But all Christians will be concerned that every piece of the vast human mosaic in their neighborhood, state, and world is discipled. They will be concerned that their church is not merely caring for itself, not merely growing by a few percentage points each year, not merely building new and beautiful buildings or having lovely worship services.

These are all good things, but in addition every church should be concerned that the tremendous number of secularists, humanists, nominal Christians, notional Christians, and non-Christians are led to the Lord. From the tremendous number of the lost at least some every year should be brought to true faith.

While not every Christian ought to be a missionary to some other people or to some other land, every Christian should help in sending missionaries, lifetime evangelists, to all undiscipled segments of mankind. All the *ethnē* in the world, whatever their language, wherever they live, whatever their income, should be discipled. Every Christian in every land should recognize this as a God-given duty.

Every branch of the universal church, every denomination, should be concerned that the billions of people now living in the world who have no contact at all with Jesus Christ, no conviction at all that Jesus Christ is their Savior and their Lord, not only hear the gospel but obey it. They should not only hear about Jesus Christ and the way to salvation but become living, devout, obedient members of Christ's family here on earth. That is what the mosaic of mankind means in terms that would be understood by all Christians in today's world.

This concept is quite contrary to the thought that many advanced Christian thinkers today hold, namely, that all men and women in the United States, Europe, Asia, Africa, and Latin America are equal. They should receive equal pay for equal work, have equal opportunities for education and advancement, and be equally influential in matters of common practice.

These seem to be attractive goals. But they do not represent the actual facts concerning today's world population. A careless thinker might maintain that entirely illiterate day laborers ought to be paid as much as finely educated professors in universities, but no government in the entire world would institute such a law. All nations and all governments, even Marxist governments, recognize that people with different abilities and responsibilities are paid at different levels.

True thinking concerning mankind must therefore always recognize that there are thousands of different pieces in the world's population. This truth is universally accepted. In theological seminaries and universities tenured professors have much greater authority and larger salaries than recently employed instructors. As we think about what Christians, seeking to be true to the Lord and to the Bible, regard as their main task, we must always see the main task as the effective discipling of tens of thousands of pieces of the human mosaic.

Furthermore, if the battle for brotherhood is to be won, we must all remember that winning men and women to faith in Christ is the longest single step we can take in that direction. Nothing we can do will move men more rapidly toward brotherhood, peace, and justice than encouraging them to become sincere, faithful, biblical Christians. If we want justice to prevail in the world, then we must carry out the Great Commission, obey eternal God's command, multiply sound Christian churches in every *ethnos* of the world.

Hispanics in the United States illustrate the challenge. There are perhaps 25 million Hispanics in this country. But Hispanics are not one piece of the mosaic. There are many kinds of Hispanics. There are fourth-generation Hispanics who speak very little Spanish. There are third generation, second generation, first generation, recent arrivals, and illegals. All of these are separate pieces of the Hispanic mosaic. Furthermore, there are Hispanics from Mexico, El Salvador, Puerto Rico, Colombia, and Argentina. All these Hispanics consider themselves distinct entities. The Hispanics from Colombia like to marry in a Hispanic community that has relatives in Colombia. Hispanics from Puerto Rico do not like to intermarry with Hispanics from Mexico. There are highly educated Hispanics fully the equal of any highly educated man or woman whose ancestors came over from Germany or England, and there are uneducated Hispanics barely able to read a word or sign their name.

The method of evangelism that will be effective in each of these segments will be somewhat different. All methods will, of course, proclaim Jesus Christ as God and only Savior and the Bible as God's Word to be obeyed. But the way in which this essential truth is proclaimed and the kind of congregations that are established will differ.

In the postwar decades of the twentieth century, when hundreds of thousands of Puerto Ricans poured into the United States, the old, well-established branches of the universal church evangelized these incoming Puerto Ricans in certain ways. They built them churches, educated their pastors, and established a few nongrowing Puerto Rican churches.

The pentecostals, however, depended on immigrants from Puerto Rico to multiply their own churches in New York. These churches were led by Puerto Ricans with relatively little education but a sound belief in Jesus Christ and the Holy Spirit. The Assemblies of God did not build churches or social service centers for those who became Christian. The new Christians rented empty stores on the less-used streets of New York. Storefront churches multiplied enormously. They were filled with rough wooden benches. On Sunday they were jammed with Puerto Ricans, hearing the Bible expounded, singing praises to God, praying in unison, and rejoicing in their Christian fellowship. The pentecostals had found a method that God was certainly blessing.

As Christians consider world evangelization, they must realize that this means precisely what the Great Commission says. It means discipling *panta ta ethnē*. It means Christianizing a multitude of pieces of the mosaic of mankind. All nations of the world are made up of many segments of humanity. Each segment, each *ethnos*, must be discipled.

We shall discuss the methods by which this may be done in the next chapter. Here we are simply making clear that the task is not to disciple nation after nation. The task is to disciple *ethnos* after *ethnos*, clan after clan, neighborhood after neighborhood, segment after segment of the vast mosaic of mankind.

Christianity will prosper, the world will become Christian, chiefly as members of all the segments of society realize that they can become Christians while remaining themselves. Each piece of the mosaic will remain a separate piece, considering itself unique.

Note that this concept is directly opposed to the concept very common in increasing measure in country after country. It is directly contrary to the idea that as Navaho Indians become Christian, they cease being Navahos and become just ordinary Christian Americans. As soon as this false idea is recognized as false, as soon as carrying out the Great Commission is taken quite literally, we shall be on solid ground. As soon as we begin to *matheteusate panta ta ethnē;* as soon as we begin to Christianize tribe after tribe, clan after clan, caste after caste; as soon as we begin to pray that God will start a movement in each piece of the mosaic, men and women while remaining in the piece of the mosaic in which they were born will also become disciples of the Lord Jesus. They will actively work so that all men and women of that tribe can become Christ-believing, saved, Spirit-filled members of his body, the church.

The mosaic of mankind must be discipled. Every piece

of the mosaic must be discipled, incorporated in the body of Christ, enrolled in Christ's school. That is the command of eternal God himself. That is what Paul so clearly tells us in 1 Corinthians 9:22 and 11:1: "I have become all things to all men that by all possible means I might save some. . . . Follow my example, as I follow the example of Christ." We must be all things to all men in order to win some. But in doing that, we must not insist that whether they like it or not, they leave their own people and join our people. As soon as we can free the Christian movement from that false idea, we will experience a tremendous surge in the growth of the church.

There are sections of many populations in which people of several different segments are coming to live together, to intermarry, to form new pieces of the mosaic. Where several elements of the population are consciously or unconsciously becoming a new people, those churches will prosper that encourage and help people of several different segments of the population to become one new population. This is happening in many parts of the United States, England, France, Australia, and in some larger cities of the third world.

However, while we recognize that this second movement is going on (that becoming Christian is helping several pieces of the mosaic to become one piece), we must always remember one thing. The way in which Christianity is and always has been multiplying most rapidly throughout the earth is for groups to become Christian while still remaining in their own piece of the mosaic. So these two systems must go side by side.

# 7

# HOW CAN AN *ETHNOS* BE DISCIPLED?

## Donald A. McGavran

In the previous chapter we saw that mankind is a mosaic. Imprinted on our minds is the fact that the population of every country is made up of many *ethnē* or mosaic pieces. We now ask a question most important to all those concerned with modern missions. How can each piece of the mosaic be won to Christ? How can the world's population (clans, neighborhoods, tribes, and castes) be discipled? This chapter will deal with two methods of evangelism —group-by-group and one-by-one.

Many Christians think that all men and women will be discipled by one or two methods. Evangelists from all branches of the universal church will proclaim the gospel. Those who hear it, believe it, and become baptized members of ongoing churches will have been discipled.

This simplistic idea is modified by the fact that each piece of the mosaic requires a somewhat different method of evangelism. The methods that would win agnostic professors in American universities (one-by-one) would prove quite useless when leading an illiterate animistic African tribe to the Christian faith (group-by-group). The methods that will disciple the rural people of Brazil will be quite different from the methods which will establish congregations in the urban areas of North America, Europe, and Asia. Again, methods that will work in a country with a state church like Norway or Spain will be different from methods that will work in countries like Canada, the United States, Zambia, or Burma, where the church exists in many branches, commonly called denominations.

David Barrett notes that in India there are 26,000 castes, each of which marries strictly within itself.[1] The methods that God will bless there will permit men and women to become Christians without rejecting their caste. This is being done on a very large scale in America, where whites can become Christian without joining a black community, and Puerto Rican Hispanics can become Christian while remaining distinctly Puerto Rican.

The vast number of different languages greatly complicates the question of methods. Where the standard language—whether French, German, English, Italian, or Finnish—has been taught for several generations to all children in schools, we could say that the gospel must be proclaimed in the national language. But in many countries each piece of the mosaic speaks a somewhat different language. Proclaiming the gospel in the national language will not really reach the people. They may know the national language, but what they think, rejoice, and sorrow in is their own local language. These local languages are sometimes dialects and sometimes distinct languages. While educated men and women in any land will assure you that everybody understands the national language, the fact of the matter is that the language that stirs their emotions and in which they make their deep decisions is their heart language.

Consequently, to be proclaimed effectively the gospel must be voiced in the heart language of the people who hear it. Uneducated women hearing it in the heart language must be just as impressed as educated leaders hearing it in the national language. Only then will families decide together to become Christian. Only then will Christianity sweep through that piece of the mosaic.

In this world there are many languages, dialects, tribes, castes, income levels, and degrees of education. There must be a method suited to each of these segments of humanity. Only then can we carry out God's command to disciple every piece of the mosaic in every country of the world.

God blesses many methods that across three or four decades will lead entire units of society to become Christian. God blesses many methods by which whole segments of a given population become disciples of the Lord Jesus. These methods are being blessed by God in many countries of the world, like Africa, China, the Philippines, and the Indian tribes in Guatemala and the High Andes. We are talking about a cluster of methods that will win large parts of each *ethnos* to the Christian faith. Let us now turn to two brief examples of group-by-group evangelization.

In 1954 in central Africa a missionary took me to meet two adjoining subtribes. The first had become solidly Christian. In the second, no one had. As we drove through the non-Christian subtribe, we were stopped in one village. The missionary entered into conversation with a crowd that gathered around the car. They declared that they were ready to become Christian because one of their young women had started living with a man from the neighboring Christian subtribe. The pagan village liked what he said about the village becoming Christian. They declared they were all ready to become Christian.

The missionary asked them five questions: (1) When I send you a pastor, will you build him a hut like your own to live in? (2) All of you will worship at night and on Sundays in a church building like your huts but much larger. Will you build it? (3) Will you send all of your boys to school, which your new pastor will conduct daily in the church house you build? (4) When you go hunting, will you bring back meat for the pastor? And will you give him land on which his wife can grow the food his family needs? (5) Will you send your best young man and his wife to Mondombe, where I live, to learn how to read and write and to become a pastor of some village of your subtribe?

They answered yes to all these questions. The missionary then wrote down one hundred or more names and drove on. That village had taken a decisive first step to becoming Christian.

I turn now to an American illustration. The Free Methodists in northeastern Indiana and southeastern Michigan have many churches, most of which are more than one hundred years old. Their members are respectable middle-class citizens. Appalachians flooded into this area in the mid-twentieth century but did not join Free Methodist churches. Why?

There are several reasons. A major one is that the Appalachians are a distinct piece of the American mosaic. When they go to middle-class and upper-middle-class churches, they do not feel at home. When they listen to sermons delivered by college and seminary graduates, they feel they are listening to a different language. The food at church suppers is not quite Appalachian food.

If churches are to multiply among the Appalachian piece of the American mosaic, they must be churches in which the Appalachians feel thoroughly at home. Most of the members will be Appalachians. The food at church suppers will be Appalachian. The sermon illustrations will sound interesting to them. The pastor will be Appalachian. So will most of the deacons and elders.

Similar illustrations could easily be cited, such as the French Canadians flooding into the northern states and the recent arrivals from Mexico, El Salvador, Guatemala, Puerto Rico, and Colombia. The vast population in China is like that of Europe. It is made up of many different pieces speaking different languages. Some Chinese speak Cantonese, others speak Hakka, Minan, Lisu, and other languages. The heart language in Chinese churches in the

United States is seldom standard Mandarin. Chinese feel at home in these churches only if they come from the same part of China, the same clans, and speak the same language.

In America one-by-one methods are highly respected. "In America," say many Christian leaders, "the church welcomes people of all sorts. In Christ there is no Jew nor Greek. We are all one new people—the people of God."

As we look at the growth of the church, however, we must always remember that while God certainly blesses the "one-by-one from many different pieces of humanity" methods, these seldom cause the church to grow greatly.

Great growth almost always comes where people of one class, one degree of wealth or education, one *ethnos*, flood into the church. When that happens, then churches really multiply.

In India when a Hindu turned to Christ as a single convert, he was invariably an outcast. People would not eat with him. They would not take water from his hands. They would not permit him to enter their houses. He was no longer one of them. He had become a sacred cow-eating Christian.

All over India churches which grew by one-by-one methods were far more numerous than churches which grew by people movements. Mass movements or people movements, as they should be called, took place in only a few mission stations.

In mid-India in 1935 there were 145 mission stations started by missionaries from England, America, Sweden, Canada, and other lands. In 134 of these the method of conversion was one-by-one. In these stations, only one or two churches were found, and these were growing very slowly. Sometimes the converts were won in the hospitals that missionary doctors had founded. Sometimes conversions took place among students who had graduated from mission schools. Occasionally they took place among those who read Christian tracts or the New Testament. Sometimes they took place as famine orphans were gathered, cared for, and fed. After the famine was over, such orphans could not return to their villages and homes, because they had eaten food prepared by Christians.

Christians in the slow-growing churches were generally well educated, and were frequently employed by the mission as evangelists, preachers, hospital workers, or in other ways. The church, established in 134 towns and cities, worshiped in church buildings erected by the missionaries. Christians did not look like Untouchables. They looked like and were in fact educated Indians.

In 11 of the 145 stations, however, there had been people movements. Sometimes these were small, involving only a few thousand people. Sometimes they were large—fifteen to twenty thousand people were involved. There had been people movements among four castes—the Balahis, the Bhils, the Garas, and the Mahars. The methods God blessed were Christian movements within castes.

In many countries of the world both people movements to Christ and one-by-one conversions to Christ can be found. Each of these clusters, of course, uses distinct methods. In some people movements the pastor is supported by the new Christians, as in the illustration from central Africa. In other places, the new congregation is pastored by a preacher supported by the mission. In still other places the pastor is supported by teaching in a school where the students pay him. God blesses many methods in both clusters. It is most important in all propagating of the gospel to find a method God will bless in the section of the population in which Christians are attempting to multiply churches.

The New Testament abundantly supports both methods. It supports one-by-one conversions. We think of the crippled man at the Beautiful Gate (Acts 3:2–8); the eunuch, baptized hundreds of miles from his home in Ethiopia (Acts 8:27–38); and Saul, the persecutor of the church, converted on the road to Damascus (Acts 9:3–18). These were unquestionably single individuals who turned from their families and close associates to embrace the Christian faith.

There were doubtless many other single conversions which
are not described in the Book of Acts.

The much more numerous examples, however, are of
groups of individuals becoming Christian. When the Lord
Jesus founded the church, eleven of his disciples were
Galileans; there was only one Judean, and he betrayed his
Lord. As Christ's church grew after Pentecost, it became a
church whose members were mostly working-class Jews.
The New Testament records no Sadducee conversion. A
few Pharisees became Christians; Paul was among them.
We read of no scribes and rabbis who became Christian.

A very powerful illustration comes from Paul's evangelistic tours in Asia Minor, Greece, and Rome. In the first
century of our era in the Grecian world there was in most
Jewish synagogues a railing halfway back. True Jews, who
were circumcised and ate no pork, sat in front of this railing. Back of the railing sat many Gentiles, who liked the
Old Testament faith, who believed that there was one God,
who liked what they read and heard from the prophets
and the psalms and the other books of the Old Testament.
But they were not quite ready to be circumcised, a painful
process, or to give up eating bacon and ham. Consequently, while they attended the synagogue, they sat back of
the railing.

When Paul spoke in the synagogues (as recounted in the
Book of Acts), he received a tumultuous welcome. Where
did the welcome come from? From people in front of the
railing or back of the railing?

While the New Testament does not say this, we are
amply justified in believing that it came mostly from people back of the railing. Some of the people in front of the
railing also believed and welcomed him. Some of the Jews
born of Jews, like Paul himself, who sat in front of the railing, believed what Paul said. But most of the people who
sat in front of the railing, most of the racially solid Jews,
did not believe his message. They said, "This will destroy
the Jewish faith." Consequently, we read frequently in Acts
that the Jews (the full Jews) chased Paul out of town. They

all but killed him on a number of occasions. But the people back of the railing and a few in front of the railing formed the house churches that multiplied during the course of Paul's ministry (Acts 13:14–16, 43; 14:1). The house churches abundantly illustrate group-by-group conversions. In short, the New Testament bears abundant testimony that God blessed both one-by-one conversions and group-by-group conversions.

As the world grows more and more populated, as transportation and radio become increasingly common, certain segments of the population begin to meld together.

When slaves were captured from many different tribes in Africa, loaded into slave ships, brought across the ocean, and sold in the Caribbean Islands or the United States, they became a new people. All memory of their tribal origins disappeared. They melded together into one new people, today called the blacks or Afro-Americans.

In all the great cities of the third world—and the first and second world also—people from varying sections of the population, from varying pieces of the mosaic, also frequently meld into new pieces.

A woman with a Scottish name will marry a man who has an Italian, German, or Chinese name. In short, some pieces of the mosaic are joining one another, are mixing together, are becoming one new people. This happens in all countries. It is particularly noticeable in places like North America.

In melding populations God blesses methods different from those he blesses where pieces of the mosaic remain quite distinct. This one-by-one plan of discipling is a good way, a God-blessed way, but it is a minor way. It will yield large growth in relatively few places. But it is nevertheless a sound way in certain sections of the population where the old lines of tribe and caste and clan and language are being eroded and a new society is being formed.

It is most important that as we carry out the Great Commission we recognize the two main clusters of methods of discipling *ethnos* after *ethnos*, two distinct ways of

carrying out the Great Commission. We must remember
that only those methods will be blessed by God which fit
the population in which they are employed. We must
disciple intelligently. We must listen to the guidance of
God in these matters. We must remember that when the
gospel was first proclaimed, the Lord Jesus Christ himself
started the church among one small segment of the human
mosaic, the Jews.

The mosaic of mankind is the reality that faces
Christians in all countries, in all continents, in all languages, in all sections of the world's population, the rich
and the poor, the educated and the uneducated, the urban-
ites and the ruralites, and every other piece of the mosaic.
As Christians evangelize, they must realize that there are
certain rules laid down in the Bible itself according to
which the gospel will prosper. Let us all remember that we
are to carry out God's command. We are proclaiming the
gospel and discipling men and women in a world where
the Bible clearly recognizes that most of this discipling is of
*ethnos* after *ethnos*.

In Matthew 28:18–19 we read that the ultimate authority
in the universe, the Lord Jesus Christ, commands that all
the *ethnē* be discipled. He did not command that all the
men and women be discipled. The Ultimate Authority recognized that the *ethnē*—pieces of the mosaic—will become
Christians while remaining themselves.

In Revelation 7:9 we read that men and women from
"every *ethnos*, tribe, people and language" will be there
before the throne. These tribes and tongues and peoples
will remain until the end. They are part of the human
order.

The methods, therefore, will be numerous. Since there
are multitudinous *ethnē*, there will be multitudinous methods. As we carry out Christ's command in the Great
Commission, we must make sure that the method we use
in a particular *ethnos* fits that *ethnos*. Only then will it be
possible to obey our Lord.

# 8

# TWENTY THOUSAND BRANCHES IN ONE UNIVERSAL CHURCH

## Donald A. McGavran

The Christian world has long been troubled by the fact that many branches of the church have considered themselves as the only true church. All other branches were regarded as cults or heresies. Each branch maintained that it was the true church. It alone had the truly correct rendition of certain passages in the Bible.

As the Western Church from the time of Paul for one thousand years spread through the various countries of western Europe, all the bishops were ordained by the bishop of Rome, who, it was claimed, was the only legitimate successor of Peter. The basic passage which Roman Catholics interpreted as supporting this doctrine is Matthew 16:16–18: "Simon Peter answered, 'You are the Christ, the Son of the living God.' Jesus replied, 'You are Peter (*Petros*), and upon this rock (*petra*) I will build my church.'" The Church of Rome believes that this passage supports its claim to be the only true church, founded on

Peter the rock. The bishop of Rome (the pope) is the ultimate authority. All other branches of the universal church,
however, maintain that the rock on which Christ builds his
church is not Peter (*Petros*) but Peter's clear statement
(*petra*), "You are the Christ, the Son of the living God."

When Luther, Calvin, and Knox, maintaining that the
Church of Rome had many doctrines that were clearly not
biblical, formed Protestant churches, each Protestant
church maintained that it was the only true church and
that Roman Catholicism was a heresy. Much of Germany,
all of Denmark, Norway, Sweden, Finland, and Scotland,
and much of England became Lutheran, Presbyterian, and
Anglican.

All kinds of new branches of the church began. George
Fox, turning again and again to the Bible, refused to call
the English Episcopal churches "churches." He called them
"steeple houses." He maintained that true Christianity
resulted from his interpretation of the Bible, his choice of
biblical passages. As a result many Quaker denominations
arose and flourished.

The Baptists, believing that the New Testament clearly
teaches baptism of repentant men and women by immersion (the Greek word *baptizō* means immersion), formed
denominations of their own. These were wiped out by the
Calvinists in Switzerland but formed small denominations
in France, Germany, Denmark, England, and Scotland.

In America the Baptists multiplied exceedingly so that
today the Southern Baptists, just one of many Baptist
denominations, with 15 million baptized believers and
probably another 15 million children of baptized believers,
form a significant part of the American population.

Much more could be written about the way in which
branches of the universal church multiplied congregations
in many pieces of the human mosaic. In 1982 there were
20,800 denominations in the world.

Even the Roman Catholic Church (which until the 1960s
maintained that it was the only true church) changed its
position in the Second Vatican Council held in Rome in

1962–65. After several paragraphs maintaining that the Roman Catholic Church is the only true church, there are several paragraphs about "separated brethren." For the first time the Roman Catholic Church admits that there are some brothers in Christ outside their church.

What must true Christians make of this situation? Sincere Christians and careful Bible students arrive at somewhat different interpretations of what the Bible says about the church. Is there just one true church, or does the church exist in many different branches?

We maintain that the universal church is indeed the body of Christ. Christ has one body, the church; there is one church. However, this does not mean and, in view of all the facts cannot mean, one human organization—the Syrian Church, the Eastern Orthodox Church, the Roman Catholic Church, the Presbyterian Church, or the Lutheran Church.

The church is the body of Christ. As the body of any person is made up of many different parts—fingernails and eyes, skin and bones, lungs and brain, blood vessels and hair, heart and liver—so the body of Christ has now and will continue to have many different parts.

The church spreads enormously in China today. It is composed of congregations that build no church buildings. The Chinese churches that have come into being in the past twenty-five years meet in homes, gardens, rented halls, school buildings, and the open air.

This is exactly what happened during the first century or two of the Christian era. Archeologists find no foundations of churches from A.D. 100. They find a few foundations from the year 200.

The New Testament churches mentioned in the epistles and Acts were house churches. When Paul writes to the church in Corinth or the church in Rome, he is writing to a group of house churches. Paul never writes saying, "When I come to Corinth, we will raise 500,000 drachmas and build a great church building at the corner of Justus and Alexander Streets."

In Romans 16:3–15, we find a long list of names. Scholars maintain that these men and women belonged to six house churches planted in Rome before Paul got there.

Does this view of the universal church destroy the conviction that the church of Jesus Christ is truly one? By no means. The church of Jesus Christ is truly one. It is the universal church, but like the body of Christ it is composed of many distinct parts.

Churches that arise in illiterate aboriginal tribes in the forests of Africa will give up their beliefs in evil spirits, gods and goddesses who live in the trees, roots, rivers, and the like. They will accept the Bible as God's Word even though only a few of them read it carefully. These branches of the church are parts of God's body. Whether they call themselves Presbyterians, Baptists, or Mennonites makes no difference as long as they believe on Jesus Christ as God and their only Savior and the Bible as the utterly true Word of God.

At the other end of the spectrum we see some congregations in the United States growing tremendously. They are also parts of the body of Christ. Hundreds and perhaps thousands of new members join them. There are congregations of three thousand, six thousand, ten thousand. The members of these churches are all educated, cultured men and women.

However, most of those who cause the growth of these churches are not converts from atheism, agnosticism, or secularism. Rather they are Christians from other branches of the church who moved into the neighborhood of the growing church. When they looked around for a new church to join, they visited several and found that the growing church had services they liked, a pastor whose style of preaching appealed to them, a building they were proud of, and a Sunday school where they wanted their children to study. So church growth came not primarily from winning modern pagans to the Christian faith but from rearranging existing Christians.

When I was in Norway a few years ago, some Lutheran

pastors were telling me that in all Norwegian state schools the children are taught the Lutheran catechism. They then go to church, are examined by the pastor, and are confirmed.

I exclaimed, "I wish this were done in North America. There any teaching of the Bible or biblical truth in public schools is forbidden."

"Well," the Lutheran pastors responded, "you must remember that the day they are confirmed in the church is for many of them the last day they ever appear in the church."

In short, how many of those who are reported by congregations and branches of the universal church as members are really practicing Christians? In fact, of the 67 percent of the English population who maintain that they are Christians, only a small portion are regular practicing Christians.

What we are maintaining is that the body of Christ must never be identified with those whose names are on some church roll. Many whose names appear on church rolls are at best notional or nominal Christians. They may have joined the church for political reasons. "Church membership enhances one's standing in the community," they may say. "I do attend now and then, especially at Christmas and Easter," they may reply. But their real religion is secularism or humanism. They really do not believe in God the Father Almighty, Jesus Christ his only Son our Savior, and the indwelling Holy Spirit. They certainly do not believe in the inspired Bible. They are inclined to believe that in the world are many religions. All have some truth in them. None of them has the complete truth.

The universal church is made up of all those who really believe on the triune God and really believe in the inspired, absolutely authoritative Bible, the Word of God—regardless of which branch of the universal church they come from. In 1982 the universal church had 20,800 branches (denominations). One hundred years from now, however, we may be sure that the number of branches in the universal church will be considerably larger.

In the 1990s as the 50 to 100 million Christians in China form themselves into new denominations, it is probable that they will not call themselves Quakers, Baptists, Episcopalians, Roman Catholics, Presbyterians, or Three Self Churches. Just what they will call themselves is not clear. We may be sure that if they really believe on the triune God, accept the Bible as their rule of faith and practice, put aside all other gods and scriptures, then God will regard them as parts of Christ's body, the universal church.

What bearing does this have on ardent Christians in the modern world? Every branch of the universal church will sincerely and faithfully teach what it believes the Bible to proclaim. If it believes that God has appointed not only deacons and elders and ministers but also bishops and archbishops and that all these offices are required by Scripture, it will certainly teach these things and will be seen by all Christians as an episcopal branch of the universal church. If, on the other hand, it believes that deacons, elders, and pastors only are appointed by God and that there is no biblical base for bishops and archbishops, it will be known as a Congregational church. If it believes that the only baptism which the Bible teaches is baptism of repentant believers by immersion, it will be known as a Baptist church. If it believes that the ultimate authority in the church is an organization of its pastors and elders called a presbytery, it will be known as a Presbyterian church.

If it believes that all congregations should be an admixture of men and women from many segments of society, it will be quite different from branches of the universal church which believe that true churches can and do arise among specific segments. These, for example, can be congregations and denominations made up exclusively of Japanese, Norwegians, or Greeks. Every branch of the universal church will sincerely and faithfully teach what it believes the Bible to proclaim.

One of the great obstacles to the growth of the church in Japan, China, Taiwan, and other east Asian countries has been that in all these countries the worship of the spirits of the ancestors was an essential part of family life. In Japan, for example, fifty years ago almost all houses had a *butsudan* near the front door. In the *butsudan*, written on small wooden slabs, were the names of the ancestors going back several generations. Devout families would make offerings to the spirits of the ancestors every day. Those who became Christian invariably removed the *butsudan* and gave up the worship of ancestral spirits. "These spirits," say the Christians, "are not gods."

All true Christians, however, do follow the biblical instruction to honor parents and other ancestors. Some have therefore suggested that in the hall of every Christian family in east Asia there should be a large white tablet on which are written the names of parents, grandparents, great-grandparents, and on and on. As members of the family enter or leave the home, they should bow respectfully before this large tablet.

Honoring ancestors is an essential part of biblical teaching. In Matthew 1 and Luke 3 the long list of names of the ancestors of the Lord Jesus Christ is abundant proof that honoring ancestors is a thoroughly Christian practice. Ancestors must not be worshiped, but they ought to be honored.

While this issue is being hotly debated in Japan and China, it is a good example of the problem discussed in this chapter. While sticking resolutely to the belief that God is one, we must realize that each segment of the population in each country will formulate doctrines that speak to its particular cultural situation. In countries where ancestors have been worshiped, they will formulate a doctrine that says, "Yes, ancestors must certainly be honored, but they must not be worshiped."

Debates of this sort have arisen, are arising, and will arise as Christianity spreads to more and more pieces of the vast mosaic of mankind.

When the Africa Inland Mission started its work in Kenya, it concentrated its efforts on the Kamba tribe. Today this 400,000-member tribe is mostly Christian. Its congregations form a new branch of the universal church, the Africa Inland Church.

When members of other tribes are evangelized by it and become Christian, should they call themselves the Africa Inland Church? Or should they call themselves by some other name and form a distinct, friendly, but separate branch of the universal church? Questions like this will arise in city after city, nation after nation, continent after continent.

Some will answer these questions by saying, no, that all new clusters of Christian congregations should belong to one universal church, which maintains that all denominations which do not belong to it are not parts of the true church. Other Christians will rejoice that the one universal church has, praise God, many glorious branches.

A most interesting illustration of the problem we are facing in this chapter comes from the great subcontinent of India with its firmly established caste system. Each caste marries strictly within itself and for the most part eats only with its own members. The caste system is based on the Hindu scriptures which maintain that god created the Brahmin castes (the highest castes) from his head. God created the Kshatriya castes from his shoulders and arms, the Vaishya castes from his thighs, and the Shudra (slave) castes from his feet. Outside the Hindu religion are the Untouchable Castes. These were the Dravidians who were conquered by the invading Aryans four thousand years ago. The Aryans regarded the Dravidians as definitely inferior, scarcely human.

There are in India today possibly 25 million Christians. Some 4 million of these are Syrian Christians—Roman Catholic Syrians, Orthodox Syrians, and Mar Thoma Syrians—who live in Kerala in the southwest tip of India. These all consider themselves upper-caste people. They are wealthy. Many of them are lawyers, doctors, merchants, large land owners, teachers, and the like. They marry only Syrians. They intend to maintain themselves as a distinct segment of the Indian Christian population. The remaining Christians in India, perhaps 20 million, with very few exceptions have grandparents or great-grandparents who are Untouchables or tribals. The only great movements to Christ in India have come from the aboriginal tribes and the Untouchable Castes.

As a result, today when Respectable-Caste Hindus (Brahmins, Kshatriyas, Vaishyas, and Shudras) hear the gospel, they find it almost impossible to become "Christians." They may believe on the Lord Jesus Christ. They may take the Bible as God's final revelation. They may heartily dislike the 330 million gods and goddesses of the Hindu religion. They may dislike the monkey-headed god Hanuman or the elephant-headed god Ganesh or the sex image of the great god Mahadeo. But they ardently maintain, "We cannot be baptized and become members of churches whose members are very largely from the bottommost castes and tribes of this great land."

The great seventeenth-century Roman Catholic missionary Robert de Nobili ruled that converts from any caste should consider themselves members of that caste, while they gave up all scriptures except the Bible and all gods except the triune God. Upper-caste converts continued to marry in their own caste. They were Christian segments of their caste just as today in Hindu India there are Marxist segments of the Respectable Castes. Many of the leaders of the Communist party in India are Brahmins (the topmost castes in India). These continue to marry only Brahmins and eat only what other members of their caste eat. Europeans in India have always married Europeans. Chinese living in India today marry only Chinese. Ao Nagas in northeast India on becoming Christian remain Ao Nagas. From de Nobili's time until 1805, the missionaries to India permitted converts from the upper castes to maintain their caste standing. Then in 1805 an Anglican bishop ruled that all Christians would renounce caste as part of becoming Christian. As a result, this became the universal rule for all missionaries from all Protestant as well as Roman Catholic missions.

There is loud dissent in India today. There is no biblical

basis for the doctrine that the first step in becoming a Christian is to give up caste. The Bible does not support the doctrine that 100 percent practice of brotherhood is an essential first step in becoming a Christian.

Brotherhood, justice, fairness, and equality are certainly biblical goals. The longest step men can take in achieving these goals is certainly to become Christian. But there is nothing in the Bible to support the position that the practice of complete brotherhood is the first necessary step in becoming Christian. Rather, it is a *fruit* of becoming Christian. Nothing will promote justice, equality, and brotherhood in India better than for large numbers of people from the Respectable Castes to become Christian while still marrying exclusively among themselves.

A Lutheran missionary in south India notes that many Respectable-Caste Hindus attend Lutheran churches but refuse baptism. He urges that this practice be recognized as thoroughly Christian. Let members of Respectable Castes become followers of the Lord Jesus Christ without being baptized. If we were to follow this Lutheran minister's advice, we could go on and say, "When three thousand men and women from some Respectable Caste are believers, let them all be baptized together. They can then find spouses from among their own people. They will continue to be members of that particular caste."

Finding the right procedure is a key issue in India today. What procedure will God the Father Almighty bless as Christians carry out the Great Commission and disciple all the castes in India? As we have already seen, in all the Bibles printed in the fifteen major languages of India, Matthew 28:19 reads, *"sab jatiyon ko chela karo."* In English this means, "disciple all the castes." If these accurate translations of the Great Commission in all the languages of India are carried out, then we shall see churches growing in every one of the 26,000 castes.

As we have already seen, the Hindu scriptures maintain that God created the high castes from his head and shoulders and the low castes and Untouchables from his feet. As the Bible becomes the ultimate authority and the Hindu scriptures are recognized as the word of the invading white Aryans and not God's Word, the above-mentioned theological foundations of caste will certainly be renounced. They are sanctified, legalized racism. On this point there can be no argument.

However, what pieces of the human mosaic in India do in regard to their intimate friends is an entirely different matter. College graduates will certainly have different groups of friends than men and women who have not graduated from primary school. Men and women who live in wealthy neighborhoods will have friends among their own neighbors. Those who grow up and live in squalid inner city neighborhoods will talk with, intermarry with, and associate with squalid inner city residents. Scheduled-Caste practicing Christians will like to belong to congregations in which Scheduled-Caste Christians are the deacons, elders, and ministers.

We may say as the gospel spreads in the one hundred thousand or more *ethnē* in the world, congregations and denominations will be formed which fit *ethnos* after *ethnos*. As soundly Christian groups multiply in many segments of a population in all six continents, brotherhood and equality and justice will become widely accepted goals toward which all classes strive.

True Christians will certainly maintain that the church of Jesus Christ is one. All Christians are parts of the true vine, which has many branches. These have been cut from many kinds of vines and grafted into the true vine. Some, therefore, will bear white grapes, some purple, some pink. Some grapes ripen early, others ripen late. As long as they remain in the vine, however, as long as they draw support from the plant securely rooted in the soil, they are true grapes. In short, the universal church has many branches. Instead of trying to form one world organization, ruled by one pope or one group of carefully chosen leaders, we must recognize and rejoice in the church, the body of

Christ, with thousands of separate parts. As long as each of these believes in the triune God and the Bible as his inspired, authoritative Word, it is a branch of the one universal church.

As multitudinous pieces of the mosaic of mankind are discipled into this one universal church, as long as each piece of that vast mosaic gives up all other gods and all other scriptures, accepts the Bible as its ultimate authority and the triune God as the Creator, Sustainer, and Savior of the world, we may be sure that God's command is being carried out and that he will bless the whole undertaking.

# PART 3

# YOUTH, WORLD MISSIONS, AND THE TWENTY-FIRST CENTURY

# 9

# PUTTING TOGETHER
# YOUR "TOOL KIT"

## Roger S. Greenway

My paternal grandfather was a carpenter. In fact, he was considered a master at his trade. It seemed there wasn't anything he couldn't build, as long as he had the right tools. As a boy, I often admired his large kit of fine tools. Grandpa had collected his tools over the years. Each tool was like a close friend, and virtually an extension of himself. Grandpa would fondly describe to me the purpose of each tool. He knew precisely how and when to use each one. He frankly admitted that without his tools, he was limited in what he could do. But with his tools, he could build beautiful, lasting things.

Paul likens himself to an expert builder (1 Cor. 3:10). The building he works to erect is the church of Jesus Christ (v. 9). The foundation of the building is none other than Jesus Christ (v. 11). Paul knew that he was not alone as a church builder. Other believers worked alongside him and many would come after him. The burning question for builders is the quality of their work (v. 13). Will their work for God's building endure, or will it fail in the time of testing?

Every person who wants to go to work for God needs to gather the right tools and become skilled in using them. By tools, I mean the personal spiritual qualities and experiences that are important in building the church. Nobody has all the tools. Nor does every Christian worker need all the tools all the time. But I promise that you will certainly need most of them, and some of them are indispensable right from the start.

For that reason, I believe that serious believers who want to be used to build Christ's church will begin early to gather the tools they need. You certainly don't want to wait until you go overseas or take up your first assignment. Secure as many tools as you can as early as you can, and begin mastering their use.

I see a disturbing number of burn-outs in Christian service. Often the burn-outs occur because workers fail to acquire the right tools, or they fail to master them before they start. Shoddy work, personal breakdowns, and early departures can generally be avoided if Christian workers prepare themselves properly and master the right tools.

Missionary service will test and stretch your resources beyond anything you expect. Even skilled workers feel the stress. You can't start too early, therefore, to build your ministry skills, experiences, and personal qualifications. If you are married, or plan to be, it's important to include your spouse in the process of mastering the necessary tools.

Basic missionary tools are as follows:

*A strong spiritual life.* This includes a disciplined devotional life of prayer and Bible reading in the fellowship of the Holy Spirit.

Mission workers tend to be activists. There are many urgent things to do, and so few workers, that the temptation is to neglect personal spiritual exercises. In a recent survey taken of missionaries in more than a dozen countries, spiritual barrenness was listed as the number one problem. Many of the missionaries admitted that their devotional habits had been poor even before coming to the field. Once they became involved in the work, things got worse.

The best advice I can give a prospective missionary is to enter missions on your knees. Missionaries are not exempt from temptation, satanic attack, depression, and fruitlessness. In fact, Satan takes special interest in attacking Christ's most active workers. Therefore, before anything else, master the tools of prayer, Bible reading, and communion with God.

*A love for people.* Christ's servant, Paul, is an example of a loving missionary. He can write to the Philippian Christians that he has them in his heart (Phil. 1:7). When he bade his last farewell to the church leaders of Ephesus, "they all wept as they embraced him and kissed him" (Acts 20:37). Paul's great love for God and people lay at the heart of his success as a church developer.

Unfortunately, some church workers prefer books to people. Others enjoy administrating, as long as they don't have to get too close to people. But mission work never prospers when such people are involved.

In Mexico, I was invited by a Presbyterian pastor to help figure out why his church's Sunday school was having so many problems. The superintendent seemed highly qualified, and in fact was a professor of education at the national university. They used the best materials, and offered a training class for teachers each Thursday evening. But the Sunday school experienced continual discord and problems.

I spent several hours with the superintendent, and finally discovered the root of the problem. "I enjoy administering the Sunday school," he told me. "Nothing pleases me more than seeing a well-organized Sunday school. But keep me away from children. I can't stand children!"

Sometimes I meet missionaries who don't enjoy mixing with people. Likewise, there are pastors who prefer the isolation of their studies to the bustle of the marketplace or the livingrooms of their parishoners. Christian work languishes under such people.

Ask God to give you great love for people of all kinds, and practice mingling with and serving a wide spectrum of people and needs.

*A basic and growing theology for missions.* A person's understanding of God—who he is, what his plan is for the world and for history, and what he expects from Christ's followers—is essential to missions.

We will never go anywhere in missions without a basic and growing understanding of God's nature and will, as revealed in Scripture. It is from Scripture that missions receives its motivation, direction, and staying power.

There are demonic forces and sophisticated religious systems waiting to bombard the servants of God who go out to bring the gospel. Besides, there are powerful movements and ideologies that can easily confuse and bewilder Christian workers who are not well anchored in God's Word.

Christian missions is so big and complex an enterprise that it tends to draw workers into many different arenas of challenge and conflict. Be sure that you take hold early of a basic, biblical theology and keep growing in it through the years.

After taking hold of it yourself, communicate that theology to others through your teaching, writing, and conversation. In that way you will make strong disciples and vital churches.

*Goals and strategies to achieve the goals.* Good carpenters don't start their work until someone has produced a plan for them to follow. Carpenters don't just nail boards together hoping that somehow a house will come out of it. They have a plan, and by following that plan they eventually produce the kind of building they want.

Christians, on the other hand, are sometimes misled into thinking that plans and goals aren't necessary in mission work. They believe that missionaries need only to plunge in, and somehow they will discover the right goals and strategies along the way. But that is foolishness. Missionaries should conduct their work with carefully chosen strategies and biblical, measurable goals.

This means that wise missionaries put in their tool kit the basic principles of time management, goal setting, and strategic thinking. By so doing, they avoid wasting time and resources. Careful planning generally produces the kind of focused mission work that God blesses with fruitfulness.

*Training and experience in the following areas:*

> *Personal evangelism.* Missionaries need to be able to present the gospel story simply and clearly, and tell their own story in terms of what the gospel means. Reciting a "canned" testimony is not enough for an effective witness to Christ.
>
> *Organized evangelism.* Besides the ability to engage in personal evangelism, the prospective missionary should gain experience in presenting the gospel through a group effort, following a common plan and sharing responsibilities in a team effort.
>
> *Small group Bible studies.* Organizing and leading small groups for evangelism and nurture is excellent training for missionaries. The small group Bible study is probably the single most effective and adaptable method for spreading the gospel in virtually any culture.
>
> *Counseling and discipling.* Inquirers and converts invariably need help in growing spiritually and dealing with the problems left over from their old life. Training and experience in counseling fledgling believers and troubled people are highly recommended assets.
>
> *Church organization and ministry.* Just as Paul was a church organizer, modern missionaries must make it their goal to establish churches wherever they are needed. A keen understanding of what the church is and how it ministers as a body are indispensable items of equipment. A prospective missionary should be part of a vital church and learn how it functions from the inside.

*Leadership development.* Following the example of the apostles, missionaries expend great effort to produce local leaders who can carry on the ministry after they depart. Leadership development is a process, with definite steps that need to be learned. *Effective ministry to the poor.* If sheer benevolence is all you have in mind, there is little you need to learn about ministering to the poor, because giving things away is relatively easy. But helping the poor to become self-sufficient is a level of charity requiring special knowledge and skill. Because missionaries often face poverty among the people with whom they work, they need to acquire a basic knowledge of development techniques and of the mistakes to be avoided.

*Cross-cultural skills.* Most mission work calls for living happily in a cultural environment different from your own. Do you possess the flexibility to adjust to another culture, and to enjoy living among people of another race?

Conducting a cross-cultural ministry has its own unique challenges. Teaching, counseling, presenting the gospel, developing leaders, and building lasting relationships with people are essential parts of a missionary's task. Success in each of them depends to a large extent on cross-cultural gifts and skills.

I have never heard of anyone suddenly receiving the necessary cross-cultural aptitudes while riding on the plane en route to the field. Therefore, before boarding the plane it would be wise to experience cross-cultural living and ministering in your home country. Big cities offer you opportunities to test whether you possess cross-cultural skills or build up the skills you already have.

*If married, a spouse who is committed to missions.* Stress and sacrifice come with missions, and both partners in a marriage need to be certain of their calling and God's will for them in missions.

Often a major source of stress comes in the area of cross-cultural living and ministering. Basic gifts and aptitudes are needed in the family, and these should be tested to a reasonable degree before going overseas.

*Leadership qualities corresponding to the assignment.* Missionaries are often expected to be "generalists," willing and able to do anything. But it is a mistake to expect people to perform effectively and happily in a role that does not match their skills and disposition. Besides the pain and discomfort, it's a serious waste of God-given resources. God made each of us different, and wise leadership takes these differences seriously when assigning missionaries to specific ministries.

Some people perform best when they are given free rein to tackle new ventures, tough challenges, and unexplored areas. Such people make great church planters. Starting from scratch and carving out a congregation where before there was nothing is the kind of challenge they like. I call them "type-1" leaders. They are the aggressive initiators. But a wise administrator does not leave them too long in a place where they have started new work because they usually are not good organizers. By nature, they are soon itching for new mountains to climb.

There are other people who work best when they have something to start with, a small group of believers whom they can strengthen, organize, and form into a church. I call them "type-2" leaders. They pick up the work where the type-1 leaders leave off and they make it into something lasting.

Then there are the "type-3" leaders, who are gifted to maintain what is already established. Most pastors represent this kind of leader, and churches need a great number of them. They come to an established group and maintain it well. When they depart, the work is as strong or stronger than when they arrived.

Now, if you try to make type-3 persons into church planters, it won't work. They will soon become discouraged. By the same token, type-1 leaders get bored quickly in maintenance roles. They want to start new things, initiate, and do what nobody has done before. Raw church planting demands a type-1 missionary, but a wise supervisor never leaves a type-1 in charge too long. Such a missionary usually lacks the patience to organize and strengthen the new group. For that role type-2 leadership is needed.

It's a serious mistake to force yourself or anyone else into roles that don't fit. If you want to serve long and fruitfully in missions, find out what type you are. There are tests you can take to discover this. Once you have analyzed yourself, search out a mission organization that can place you in the kind of ministry that fits your gifts and personal make-up.

Remember this: God made you a certain way, and you are one of his precious resources for carrying out his will. So find a place on the field that matches your gifts and aptitudes.

*Acquaintance with mission literature and the major areas of challenge in the world.* William Carey, founder of modern missions, studied world maps, explorers' reports, and the accounts of mission work among American Indians as part of his preparation for going to India. Far more information is available today than Carey could have dreamed of. But the basic principle remains the same.

Acquaint yourself with books and reports that can shape your understanding of effective evangelism and mission work, the kind that results in people being drawn to Christ and churches multiplied. Identify the most needy areas of the world, and where and how the Spirit is working to expand the church. Then prayerfully consider where you should invest your life and energies.

*An adventuresome spirit.* Besides possessing a contagious enthusiasm for the Lord, the gospel, and people, missionaries need an adventuresome spirit. They must be flexible and willing to experiment, try new things, and take risks. Timid hearts don't last in missions.

In *Why Settle for More and Miss the Best?* Tom Sine calls for a "renaissance of Christian imagination in life and missions."

"God isn't looking for the luminaries—the prestigious and the powerful—to advance His cause," says Sine. "He is looking for ordinary people like you and me. He invites you and me to the extraordinary adventure of seeing the world changed."[1]

God has called us to live and work for him in the closing decade of the second millennium since Christ's birth. Some of us may still be serving him when the third millennium begins. What a privilege—to be servants of God, builders employed in the greatest program on earth!

You should carefully put together your "tool kit," making sure that every item you will need is included and that you are growing in your ability to use every tool skillfully.

# 10

## HELPING AND HARVESTING THE POOR AND THE LOST

### Roger S. Greenway

I have three major concerns as I look around the world today. I think they represent the biggest challenges facing Christians at this time. The more I investigate these three concerns, the more I realize that they are intimately related. I doubt that we'll find a solution to any one of them without dealing adequately with the other two.

First, there are several billion human beings on this planet who are, by the Bible's definition, spiritually lost. Some of them adhere to an organized, non-Christian religion such as Hinduism or Islam. A growing number are taken in by the New Age movement, which presents a radically different vision of God, the world, and the purpose of life. But whatever their religion is called, we can only say that people whose faith is essentially different than the message of the Bible worship something other than the one true God. Their faith is not in the one and only Savior, Jesus Christ. Consequently, they have no real hope of eternal salvation.

The ten most populous countries with the largest number of non-Christians are China, India, the Soviet Union, Indonesia, Japan, Bangladesh, Pakistan, Vietnam, Nigeria, and Thailand. All of these, except Japan and the Soviet Union, have alarming poverty conditions as well.

I am deeply concerned about lost people, whatever their social status, nationality, or religion may be. I believe that God is concerned about them too.

Second, I am concerned about the more than one billion human beings who are desperately poor, who lack money and other resources to meet their basic needs. Most of the poor once lived in rural areas. Now they are often massed together in city slums and ghettos.

Most of the poor are illiterate. Hard as they try, they are powerless to escape their miserable condition. Although their numbers are large, nobody listens to them. They expect to be trampled on and usually are. Desperation leads some of them to violence and revolution.

The World Bank calls a high percentage of them the "absolute poor." The absolute poor have an income level so low that they cannot afford to buy food of sufficient quantity and quality to maintain even minimum standards of health and well-being.

Absolute poverty stands for a condition of life marked by malnutrition, illiteracy, disease, and early death. It lies below any reasonable definition of human decency. It grieves me deeply, and I believe it grieves the heart of God.

My third major concern is secularism, which I roughly define as indifference to God, religion, and the church. Although Christianity is expanding in much of the southern hemisphere, overall church membership is shrinking at the rate of fifty thousand people per week in Eastern and Western Europe, Commonwealth countries, and North America. In large areas of the world that once were centers of Christianity, secularism has torn enormous numbers of people from the churches. Now non-Christian religions, like Islam, are seeking to fill the religious vacuum. Not without reason, some Christian thinkers are calling for the reevangelization of the West.

It seems to me that Christian missions must constantly keep in mind these three harsh realities: much of the world is spiritually lost, much of the world is desperately poor, and in some places that once were Christian, the strength of the church has eroded.

The fact is that there are enormous vacuums in the world that are waiting for someone, or some movement, to fill them. The question is, who will get to those vacuums first?

In a fascinating article entitled "Where Are the Poor and the Lost?" Bryant L. Myers describes research conducted recently by World Vision International. The purpose of the research was to find out the location of the poorest of the poor and information concerning their material and spiritual condition so that a mission strategy to reach them could be designed.[1]

"The poor and the lost" is shorthand for those people who have great physical needs and also need to hear the Good News about Christ. Sometimes they are referred to as "the poorest of the poor." They are the world's most needy people.

Besides looking for the usual types of data concerning malnutrition, illiteracy, infant mortality, and food production, the research used four indicators to determine the spiritual needs of the people who were studied and their openness to hearing the gospel: (1) the percentage of active Christians compared to adherents of other religions; (2) the potential for gospel proclamation, based on a variety of measurements; (3) external barriers to the gospel, such as a lack of religious liberty and the religion or ideology of the government; and (4) the strength of the national church, the availability of Scripture, and the availability of missionary visas.

The research brought to light the fact that, generally speaking, the lost are the poor, and the poor are the lost. The people suffering the most serious physical need also have the greatest need of hearing the gospel of Jesus Christ. In addition, they are generally living in countries dominated by Marxism or Islam. These are countries that generally do not welcome missionaries, and gaining access to their people demands "creative" approaches.

Myers and his associates recognize that research of the kind they conducted must be used with discretion, and that it lacks some of the precision of most sociological research. Nevertheless, the results of their study produce a general profile of the world's spiritual and physical needs.

Mission strategists will find this information useful for developing a global perspective of the missionary task. Inherent in the data are clear hints regarding the kinds of mission strategy that are most appropriate for the world in which we live.

Examine the following data regarding the countries with the most "empty stomachs," and try to picture in your mind where these countries are located. What are the dominant religions of these countries?

- The five countries with the largest number of "absolute poor" are China, India, Bangladesh, Indonesia, and Pakistan.
- The five countries with the highest percentage of absolute poor are Bangladesh, Burkina Faso, Burundi, Haiti, and Papua New Guinea.
- The five countries having the lowest GNP per capita of population (less than $150 per year) are Chad, Ethiopia, Nepal, Burkina Faso, and Bhutan.
- The five countries where 20 percent of the population receives less than 2.5 percent of the income are Botswana, Brazil, Iraq, the Philippines, and Jamaica.
- The five countries with the highest infant mortality rate are Afghanistan, Mali, Mozambique, Angola, and Sierra Leone.[2]

The poor, of course, are not limited to these countries. They are everywhere, even in affluent nations, and no nation can claim to have solved the poverty problem. Yet a pattern emerges. Islam and Marxism are strong in countries with large numbers of poor. Political freedom is often limited and evangelizing missionaries face refusal or difficulty in obtaining visas. In none of the poorest countries is evangelical Christianity the predominant religion. The need is great; the barriers are many.

Among the unreached and unevangelized in the world, the poor represent the largest single block. Besides their spiritual condition, severe poverty is the "common denominator" that characterizes this enormous part of humanity.

Therefore, the Good News we proclaim must make sense to the poor. The poor have eyes as well as ears. They watch what we do even more than they listen to what we say. Because survival is their primary concern, our presentation of the gospel must be seen as offering some hope for the here and now as well as for eternity.

Hope in Christ needs to be communicated by loving words and deeds. When hope is preached and demonstrated, the poor see and hear the message of Christ and a sign of God's transforming love is established among them. Jesus himself ministered in that way, and we should constantly be learning from his example.

The first thing that's important for mission strategies is conformity to God's revelation in the Scriptures. Good strategies are based on the Bible, and anything in missions that is contradicted by Scripture must be thrown out.

Second, good mission strategies take seriously the realities of the world in which we operate. Given the conditions that we have reviewed, our mission strategies must address the twin problems of empty stomachs and empty souls, plus in some cases the added difficulty of restricted access in terms of missionary visas.

Conditions call for holistic mission strategies that integrate social ministries with the discipling of the poor and the multiplication of vital, ministering congregations among them. An essential part of their growth in Christ will be shown by their reaching out to their neighbors with the same kind of holistic witness that first attracted them to Christ and to membership in the church.

Social service without the proclamation of the gospel and the gathering of believers into churches will not do. The Bible never separates them and neither should we. Nor can we ignore the needs of the poor by engaging exclusively in "words-only" evangelism, without compassion demonstrated by our deeds. And we cannot allow political and religious fences to prevent us from carrying out the Great Commission. Finding and implementing creative strategies appropriate to each of these challenges are all part of missions. When the Lord says, "Go!" nothing should deter us.

Empty stomachs and empty souls are major parts of the world's problem. But in the worldwide Christian church we face a third serious concern and it is, as I said earlier, the erosion of faith and of respect for the organized church.

On the basis of Scripture, I believe that the organized church, with its members and leaders, is a God-ordained institution. Membership in the church is not an option, but an essential part of Christian discipleship.

Along that same line, I consider church planting, church development, and church renewal essential to mission strategy. Any mission strategy that does not have as its goal the planting and growth of churches is a dubious one. New Testament missions is church-planting missions.

From my point of view, any form of "churchless" Christianity is something spurious, unbiblical, and empty. It's impossible to read the New Testament, with its record of the ministries of the apostles, without seeing how important they viewed the growth of churches. That vision needs to be reinforced today.

Secularism's general indifference toward religious beliefs, values, and worldview, and its frequent hostility toward the organized church make secularism an avowed enemy of biblical missions. Secularism aims at forcing religious people out of the public arena, stranding the church on the social margins, and denying Christians the freedom to speak from faith on education, politics, justice, morality, and the marketplace.

Secularism is particularly concerned to prove that evangelical Christianity has nothing worthwhile to offer as far as providing solutions to the world's serious problems. Secularism wants to keep religion private, bland, and innocuous. An evangelical faith that is vigorously proclaimed and coupled with a vibrant social concern is the farthest thing from secularism's portrayal of Christianity, or of the way secularists want Christians to behave.

One way to pull the fangs of secularism is to engage in holistic missions, tending to the needs of the poor while at the same time preaching the gospel and multiplying churches among them. When Christians neglect that triad, they leave themselves vulnerable to secularism's attack. Keeping them together silences the enemy and addresses the needs of both the poor and the lost.

Harvesting the fields of the spiritually lost and helping the poor and needy converge at the point where church planting and community development meet. They are like a two-edged sword.

The thing to see is that the needs of the poor are spiritual as well as material. In fact, the gift of new hope, faith, and ideas is the greatest of all. The poor person's lack of hope is even more debilitating than the lack of wealth.

It is the gospel of Jesus Christ that offers the poor person the faith, values, discipline, hope, and motivation that are the springboard of change and transformation. At this point, the role of the church is crucial. Wherever the church is planted and the full message of the Bible is taught with vigor, the task of the social worker is made easier. Faith in Jesus Christ, instruction in the Scriptures, and the impulses of the Holy Spirit give the poor person the new outlook, motivation, and value system that are the underpinnings of community development.

The ultimate goal of Christian community development is for people to become free in Christ and under the guidance of his Word and Spirit to serve as salt and light (Matt. 5:13–16) in their communities. Hence, the role of the church in the communities of the poor is obvious.

Instead of isolating itself and ignoring social conditions that degrade and destroy human life, the church should see its main duty as being the spiritual home and educator of messengers of life. The church is in the business of developing new people in Christ, people who possess a radically changed worldview, ideas, values, and attitudes. Because of the changes Christ works in them they become participants in and motivators of change in the community.

The changes are personal and profound, and they affect everything. They benefit church members and the total community. The faithful church, like its Lord, defines its ministry in the community as coming to seek, to serve, and to save the hurting and lost. What better thing could happen than if, across the world, in countless poor communities, vital Christian churches like these would be planted and developed!

The burning need of the hour in missions, as I see it, is to light one million candles—call them churches—in the slums and ghettos and villages of the poor, and coupled with the skills of literacy and community development workers, teach the faith, values, and attitudes of the Word of God.

If this were done, social transformations would be bound to come. The relief of suffering has invariably resulted where new life in Christ is born, vital churches are established, and new opportunities are introduced through education and fresh resources.

Where that happens, secularism's accusation that the church has no relevance for the poor and suffering is answered flat out. And heaven rejoices when the harvest is enriched.

# 11

# YOUNG PEOPLE'S CONTRIBUTION TO WORLD MISSIONS

## John E. Kyle

Over the years I have had a continual interest in young adults. While a missionary, I spent considerable time with students on college and high school campuses as well as with young working adults sharing my concern for world missions.

Eventually it was my privilege to serve students on hundreds of college and university campuses as the mission director of InterVarsity Christian Fellowship. One of the responsibilities I had was to be intimately involved with the direction of the Urbana '79, '81, '84, and '87 Student World Missions Conventions. A total of nearly seventy thousand delegates attended.

I am concerned for your age group because you are the group most likely to go overseas to become missionaries. You will do the hands-on work "in the trenches." You are generally idealistic, optimistic, committed, and flexible, which are characteristics needed by Christians who enter cross-cultural ministries. You generally learn new languages and adapt to new customs and cultures more quickly than older people, and you usually have a whole lifetime to devote to such ministry. You probably have a good education. By world standards, you have an excellent education! You enjoy good health, and if you are committed to serving Jesus Christ, the recruitment staffs of mission-sending agencies certainly will want to talk to you. There is presently a need for at least one hundred thousand career missionaries.

If you are single or married with no children, you can travel lightly. Organizations such as Operation Mobilization (OM) and Youth with a Mission (YWAM) have grown rapidly because they challenge young adults to come and join them in the adventure of reaching the world's peoples for Jesus Christ. The salaries are low, guarantees of comfort are nonexistent, the need for mobility is high, and the commitment to Christ must be complete. Organizations like OM and YWAM are recruiting keen, highly qualified Christians from around the world to join their ranks. The same challenge is available to you to "rough it" for Christ. Thousands of your peers have accepted the challenge, and you can join them.

Christians who engage in world missions must be able to adapt to the continually changing face of the world. I expect there will be tremendous changes in the next twenty-five years. New challenges and opportunities will face us, and we must be ready. Ten years ago no one would have believed Christians would be using their English language skills to teach English as a second language in the Peoples Republic of China. Nor did anyone expect that there would be opportunities to spiritually and openly assist the people of Eastern Europe. Yet these things are happening, and I sense that with the recent changes of leadership in the communist world, additional opportunities may open up in places previously closed to Christian missions.

You may want to consider going abroad as a "tent-making" missionary, utilizing your professional skills and education to support yourself financially while witnessing for

Christ. Through this method you may be able to enter nations that are impossible for traditional missionaries to enter. Besides providing a creative way to enter semiclosed countries, tent making will probably help swell the missionary ranks in countries that are open to missionaries.

Your age group will continue to adapt easily to the unreached people strategy, to team ministries, and eventually assist in forming mission teams made up of multicultural peoples instead of American or British teams.

High levels of adaptability to new strategies for reaching the world for Christ will be absolutely necessary for future missionaries, and you young people are the most adaptable part of the adult population. Think of this: Since the time of Christ, there have been nearly 800 known strategies for evangelizing the world. Today there are at least 275 such plans earmarked to be completed by A.D. 2000. Fifty of them are actually in motion. Young, flexible Christians can identify new strategies that challenge traditional thinking about missions.

In the decade ahead you will see the progressive expansion of mission programs and organizations based in third world nations. Churches in Asia, Africa, and Latin America are in the process of forming their own mission-sending agencies in order to send their Christian youth overseas as career missionaries.

Today's Christian leaders are eagerly looking for the youth who will become the future leaders of the forces involved in world evangelization. For example, in the summer of 1988, 300 carefully selected young leaders from many nations of the world gathered in Singapore to share and discuss missions together. Another such leadership conference was held in Washington, D.C., in the summer of 1989 where nearly 1,500 potential Christian leaders came together. Everywhere it is recognized that the future leadership of world evangelization is right now being recruited to enter overseas missionary service.

Many young adults are presently working on staffs of parachurch organizations in North America. They are gaining expertise in evangelism and discipleship that can be applied to cross-cultural church-planting activities overseas under the guidance of mission-sending agencies. These potential church planters are working for such organizations as Campus Crusade for Christ, the Navigators, InterVarsity Christian Fellowship, and other campus ministries where evangelism and discipleship skills are being sharpened in practical day-to-day ministry. They can be joined by other young men and women who have been exercising similar gifts while serving in denominational or independent churches. If you fit one of these categories, you can be high on the recruiting lists of mission-sending agencies involved in church-planting ministries overseas where keen evangelists and disciplers are top priority.

It has almost always been young adults whom God has used to make extraordinary strategic changes in the course of world missions. Count Ludwig Zinzendorf of Germany was born in 1700 and converted to Christ at the age of ten. While a teenager he joined five other boys at a college in Paris to form the Order of the Grain of Mustard Seed to carry the gospel to the lost of the world. One of the boys was Peter Heiling, who eventually went to Egypt and Abyssinia and translated the Bible for twenty years before being martyred. Zinzendorf eventually formed the Moravian Church in 1727 that sent out the first Protestant missionaries and eventually sent 2,158 of its members overseas.

In 1883 seven of Cambridge University's finest students were enlisted by Hudson Taylor, the founder of the China Inland Mission, to go with him to China as missionaries. One of these young men was C. T. Studd, a champion cricket player. He divested himself of nearly all of his money before sailing for China. Studd and the other students traveled all over Britain sharing the cause of world missions before sailing to China in 1885. Soon after they left, another one hundred young missionaries sailed for China to join Studd and the others.

The Haystack prayer movement began in 1806 when five young college students on the campus of Williams College in Massachusetts gathered together to pray outside. They were caught in a rainstorm and retreated under a haystack where they prayed for world missions. Samuel Mills was their leader that day. He prayed concerning their united desire to reach the lost for Christ: "We can do this if we will!" Within three years they petitioned their denomination to form the first North American overseas board to send missionaries and soon some were sent to Hawaii. Mills went on to help form the American Bible Society and a mission to sailors in New York, worked in the inner city of New York, and ministered to Indians in Mississippi Valley. He died at sea at the age of thirty-five on a trip to assist in founding what would eventually be the nation of Liberia, West Africa.

The Student Volunteer movement was founded by college students and young YMCA-oriented people in 1888. This movement grew out of a month-long conference held by Dwight L. Moody for 251 students from across North America. At the close of the conference, 100 of the men present had volunteered for personal involvement in world missions. At one time over 40,000 students from 700 institutes and colleges were involved in the movement. By 1945, the movement had sent over 20,500 career missionaries overseas serving under a great number of different mission-sending agencies and boards. To back up these thousands of missionaries at one time were over 90,000 laypeople who were part of the Student Volunteer movement. Among the young men who helped start the Student Volunteer movement were outstanding Christians such as John R. Mott, Robert E. Speer, Luther Wishard, and Robert Wilder. They later became the outstanding leaders of the worldwide missions movement and YMCA's outreach for Christ's sake around the world.

William Cameron Townsend went to Guatemala in 1916 as a teenager to sell Spanish Bibles. He stayed to translate the entire Bible for a tribal group of Indians, which he did in eleven years. While still a young man, he helped found Wycliffe Bible Translators which today has more than six thousand missionaries serving in over thirty-seven nations doing Bible translation work in order to give forgotten, unreached groups of peoples God's Word in their own language. As a result of these translations, churches are planted and people grow in their faith in Jesus Christ.

Many other young adults could be named who have made great contributions to the cause of world missions. However, it is good to recall that the Son of Man, our Lord Jesus Christ, was only about thirty years of age when he began his formal ministry here on earth. All Christian young people should take heart when they remember that their Savior also became the greatest missionary who ever lived. He began what we now call the missionary movement when he turned over the winning and discipling of the world's people to his disciples. God entrusted to his own Son the fearsome responsibility to mobilize and train others to bring future generations into an eternal relationship to himself.

The world is still waiting for people who are willing to trust Jesus Christ with all they have. These people will be known for "turning the world upside down" for the glory of God. Some Christians feel that worldwide revival in the Christian church is overdue and will occur in the near future. The year A.D. 2000 looms ahead as not a mystical date but a prime marker in the history of the world. It positions the possibility of millions of people alive today being reached with the gospel of Jesus Christ.

It is my prayer that people of your generation who begin their careers as missionaries in the days ahead will see the need to cooperate. To cooperate will hasten the work if it is centered around three convictions: (1) the Bible is God's Word; (2) the "fields are white unto the harvest"; and (3) salvation is only by faith in Jesus Christ as Savior and Lord.

The key to carrying out the Great Commission effectively during this decade and into a new century will be cooperation between mission-sending agencies holding firmly to those three concepts and working in ways that enhance each other's ministries throughout the world. You and your peers are the key to such a partnership in the greatest cause the world has ever seen.

# WHAT'S AHEAD ON THE MISSIONARY AGENDA?

## Roger S. Greenway

Most of you will reach the peak of your careers in the twenty-first century. In this final chapter I urge you to consider the future of Christian missions, focusing on specific areas that are already forcing their way onto the missionary agenda.

As you read, I ask you to be sensitive to the Spirit's proddings and to consider investing your gifts and energies into the missionary agenda.

### Reaching Young People and Children

Today's and tomorrow's world is an amazingly youthful one. That fact must be taken into consideration in our missionary plans and operations. Every ten seconds a child is born somewhere in the world. Three and a half billion births will occur between 1980 and the year 2000, at which time half of the world will be under twenty-one years of age.

This "small half of the world" demands attention. There aren't enough evangelism materials, missionary organizations, programs, and strategies designed for children and youth. Our goal should be that every child in every city, town, and village be exposed to Christian teaching so as to have a basic understanding of what Christianity is about before reaching adulthood.

As in China, youth move the world. Politicians, educators, economists, and business leaders must take seriously what young people are looking for. The same is true in missions. In some moderately resistant populations, college and university students are proving to be the most responsive to the gospel. In strongly resistant countries, such as Japan, college students are almost the only receptive groups. Everywhere in the world, reaching young people for Christ is high on the missionary agenda.

## Linking Mass Media Evangelism to Church Growth

In Mexico City some years ago, I worked with students starting new churches in the squatter settlements that encircled the metropolitan area. The slum population was surprisingly receptive to the gospel, and we started more than two dozen churches.

We discovered that the membership of these new groups consisted of three types of believers: new converts, won by the efforts of our workers; believers from the villages who had recently migrated to the city and had not yet affiliated with a city church; and "media seekers," those people who already had a Bible or New Testament and knew a good deal about the evangelical message, but had never been personally discipled or invited to be baptized and join an evangelical church.

This alerted us to the fact that a tremendous harvest of seeking men and women is liable to be lost if more isn't done to bring media listeners and readers into personal contact with churches where they can be ministered to and guided into membership.

Billions of dollars are spent each year on mass media evangelism, ranging from radio and television to books, tracts, recordings, and Bibles. In view of the huge populations to be reached, these mass media projects are highly important. Yet more must be done to link mass media approaches to missions with the multiplication and growth of churches. There are effective ways to use mass media to stimulate church growth and penetrate areas where church planters "on foot" have not, or cannot, reach.

In the years ahead, more and more missionaries will need to be assigned to mass media evangelism. Likewise, more local churches and their members must be trained and enlisted in mass evangelistic enterprises. This is a high-priority item on the missionary agenda.

Many congregations can be begun by mass media, but only if the media says:

> Start practicing your new faith at once. You believe in God the Father Almighty and in Jesus Christ, his only Son. Put aside all other scriptures. Put aside all other gods, all idols, all pictures. Then, in your own house, start a regular worship service to which you will invite your friends.

Remember that all the churches in the New Testament were house churches. Paul never built a single building. Many great movements have started, are starting, and will start without first erecting their own buildings. The Christian movement must use this as one of its principal means of expansion.

## Penetrating "Creative Access" Countries

At the beginning of his challenging book, *God's New Envoys*, Japanese mission strategist Tetsunao Yamamori presents this advertisement:

**WANTED:**
100,000 new envoys
to serve in countries
closed to missionaries.

No salary. No security.
Hardship, danger expected.
Special training, new strategies required.

**Immediate Need!**

Yamamori estimates that when the twenty-first century begins, 83 percent of the world's non-Christian population will reside in countries closed to traditional missionary approaches. He calls for a "new breed" of missionaries —God's new envoys—who will create and carry out new strategies to reach these billions of "unreachable" people.[1]

The need for traditional missionaries will continue for years to come. But alongside them, new kinds of missionaries must be found who will commit themselves, heart and soul, to evangelizing the inaccessible people of this world.

By inaccessible people we mean people living in countries like Afghanistan, Algeria, Angola, Bulgaria, Burma, China, Egypt, Ethiopia, Cambodia, Malaysia, Saudi Arabia, Turkey, Vietnam, and many others that are largely closed to missionaries.

The alarming news is that the number of countries refusing to grant missionary visas is increasing. Some countries that traditionally were open to missionaries are beginning to impose restrictions on missionary activities.

Yet the good news is that despite government restrictions, many of these countries can be penetrated with the gospel by unconventional methods and by envoys of Christ willing to take risks, face dangers and frustrations, and implement new strategies. For that reason we call them "creative access" countries.

In Seoul, South Korea, I saw a large sign in front of a Presbyterian church. The sign read: "Wanted: 100 Kamakazi Soldiers for Jesus Christ." I was told that the church had as its goal the recruitment, training, and sending out of one hundred South Korean missionaries who will slip into closed countries in order to spread the gospel. Once sent out, these missionaries will probably never return home. They will receive and write no letters or prayer cards, nor will they ever present films or promotional literature regarding their work. They are to witness to Christ and serve the gospel until death in the land to which they are sent.

What a challenge!

"How many have responded?" I asked. "Many," they told me. "They'll send one hundred, and probably more."

## Multiplying Churches in Cities

We are living in the middle of the greatest population shift in human history. People around the world are moving from farms and villages to exploding urban centers. In the decade of the 1980s alone, it is estimated that one billion people (20 percent of the earth's population) migrated to cities. The world has become predominantly urban.

Think of this: In 1900 there was one city with 5 million inhabitants. By 2000, there will be sixty-five such cities. Today, six cities have 20 million or more inhabitants, while many others have 10 million or more.

This massive trek to the cities is linked to the population explosion that is occurring in the developing countries of Asia, Africa, and Latin America. In many of these countries the supply of jobs, homes, and other basic necessities will have to double in the next two decades just to meet the needs of people already born.

Help of many kinds is needed by people caught in the agony of urban slums and squatter settlements. Ultimately, their greatest need is to hear the gospel of Jesus Christ. The encouraging news about urbanization is that newcomers to the city generally show an increased openness to the gospel. For many of them, coming to the city means they are free for the first time to read the Bible, attend a Christian meeting, and take the gospel seriously.

Countless opportunities are waiting in the cities for Christians who want to demonstrate compassion, proclaim Christ, and gather new believers into churches. Some of us feel that God will use this massive migration to the city to provide Christian missions with history's greatest opportunity to draw people of all tribes and races to Jesus Christ and multiply churches among them.

## Ministering Holistically among the Poor

Christians with compassion and skills for helping the poor will be needed in great numbers in the decades ahead. Some countries will be closed to all missionaries except those who can offer tangible benefits to the poor and suffering.

Think for a moment about the size and significance of this challenge. By the year 2000, another billion people will be added to the earth's population. More than 90 percent of this population increase is occurring in Asia, Africa, and Latin America, areas already plagued by poverty and underdevelopment.

Of the 5.3 billion people in the world today, more than 2 billion are malnourished. Roughly 500 million of these are on the edge of starvation. In many of the world's largest cities, more than 50 percent of the people live in slums and squatter settlements.

It is estimated that 75 percent of the people of the world who are unreached by the gospel and outside the organized church are counted among the poor and suffering. That being the case, ministering for Christ among the poor figures large in the missionary agenda. More than ever before, the world needs men and women who minister in Christ's name, combining saving words with wise and compassionate ministries.

## Encountering Adherents of Other Religions

Also high on the missionary agenda is the encounter between Christians and adherents of other faiths. One-half of the human race follows some other religion. One-quarter has become highly secular and follows no religion at all. The remaining one-quarter is composed of those who call themselves Christian, although many of these are highly nominal. The non-Christian half and the secular-humanist quarter grow larger every year.

As immigrants and refugees pour into Western countries from parts of the world where non-Christian religions predominate, church members in the West encounter more and more people of other religions. Are Western Christians prepared to meet the newcomers with love and the gospel? Are churches and mission agencies actively seeking to win the newcomers to Christ and the church?

By their engagement with followers of other religions, Christians in the West share responsibility for missionary witness with branches of Christ's church in other parts of the world. Christians in Asia and Africa, for example, often find it difficult to penetrate the other religions. They are tempted to isolate themselves in Christian ghettos with little to say of a missionary nature to other religionists.

Yet the responsibility to proclaim the gospel of Jesus Christ is a global one. Solidarity with the worldwide church in faith, love, and mission points to an increasing involvement by Western churches in the life-and-death struggles against idolatry and opposition that are the common experience of many non-Western churches.

This dimension of the missionary enterprise, encountering the great non-Christian religions, is just now taking shape as the great spiritual battlefield of the future. It occupies a large place in the global missionary agenda.

## Enlisting the Gifts and Services of All God's People

It's amazing to see the rich and varied gifts God's Spirit distributes among his people. All these gifts are intended to exalt Jesus Christ and advance his kingdom in the world.

Recently I watched a team of Christian actors and musicians perform on the streets of Amsterdam. They were part of Youth with a Mission (YWAM), an evangelistic mission that has one of its centers in that European city.

Their street theater held the attention of a lunch-hour audience of more than one hundred people for nearly half an hour. They dramatized a contemporary story easy to relate to and that drove home God's message of forgiveness and hope. These young people had talent. They were skilled communicators and they were filled with the Christian message.

If the church really wants to communicate effectively to a world of busy and indifferent people, it is imperative that it make greater use of the varied gifts and resources God's Spirit makes available. The church must break its dependence on full-time salaried missionaries and evangelists because there will never be enough money to pay all the workers needed to evangelize the world.

Unpaid volunteers, bivocational missionaries, and professionals who support themselves while using their unique gifts to communicate the gospel in creative ways will be needed in large numbers if the task of world evangelization is going to be completed.

We who write this book will in all likelihood complete our missionary service within the bounds of the twentieth century, or close to it.

Yours will be the twenty-first century with all its challenges. You will face a world of teeming populations, ominous religious and political forces, and overwhelming spiritual and physical needs.

To address what lies ahead in obedience to Christ's commission will require commitment, sacrifice, and perseverance in unprecedented measure.

Keith Parks, president of the foreign mission board of the Southern Baptist Convention, puts the challenge this way:

> In the days ahead, Christians will be challenged to run risks never run before. The course ahead is uncharted. None of us has been this way before.
> The day has come to be bold without being brash; full of faith without being overconfident: Servants first, and also leaders.[2]

In the years before you, you will wrestle with questions the church never talked about before. Issues that formerly were ignored will be high on your agenda. You will have to be bold and full of faith, and more dependent upon the power of God than any generation before you. Hanging in the balance will be the temporal and eternal well being of multitudes of people.

Will zeal for missions fade as the century closes and the powers of secularism pervade the Western world? I don't believe it for a moment. We stand not at the sunset, but the sunrise of world evangelization. This is God's *kairos*, his moment to move climactically in missions throughout the world. And it is your *kairos* also, your moment in God's plan and purpose to pray and to work for the extension of Christ's kingdom.

# NOTES

## Introduction

1. John R. Mott, *The Pastor and Modern Missions: A Plea for Leadership in World Evangelization* (New York: Student Volunteer Movement for Foreign Missions, 1904), chap. 5.

## Chapter 2

1. A helpful source for this and other ideas found in chaps. 2–3 is Arthur T. Pierson, *The Divine Enterprise of Missions* (London: Hodder and Stoughton, 1892), pp. 104ff.

2. Jonathan Chao, "Evangelization in Sufferings," *World Evangelization* (Feb. 1989): 7.

3. Pierson, *Divine Enterprise of Missions*, p. 129.

4. Ibid., pp. 129–31.

## Chapter 3

1. Robert McQuilken, *The Great Omission* (Grand Rapids: Baker, 1984), pp. 11–12.

2. George F. Vicedom, *The Mission of God* (St. Louis: Concordia, 1965), p. xi.

3. This approach was introduced a century ago by Arthur T. Pierson in lectures on missions presented at the Theological Seminary of the Reformed Church in America, New Brunswick, N.J., and to the general public in the winter of 1891. Pierson later published the material in *The Divine Enterprise of Missions*.

## Chapter 4

1. Peter Wagner, *On the Crest of the Wave* (Ventura, Calif.: Regal, 1983).

## Chapter 5

1. This bibliography is available upon request from InterVarsity Missions, 6400 Schroeder Road, Madison, WI 53707.

2. This material has been prepared in videotape format by David Bryant, Concerts of Prayer International. It is available from Gospel Light Publications, Ventura, Calif.

3. Current lists of such opportunities are available from InterVarsity Missions.

4. Information about this ministry is available from International Students, Inc., Colorado Springs, Colo.

## Chapter 7

1. David Barrett, *World Christian Encyclopedia* (Nairobi: Oxford University Press, 1982), p. 230.

## Chapter 9

1. Tom Sine, *Why Settle for More and Miss the Best?* (Waco, Tex.: Word, 1986), p. xvi.

## Chapter 10

1. Bryant L. Myers, "Where Are the Poor and the Lost?" *Together* (Oct.–Dec. 1988): 8–10.

2. Tom Houston, "Good News for the Poor," address presented for Lausanne II, Manila, July 1989.

## Chapter 12

1. Tetsunao Yamamori, *God's New Envoys: A Bold Strategy for Penetrating Closed Countries* (Portland, Oreg.: Multnomah, 1987), pp. 14–15.

2. Keith Parks, *World in View: Global Evangelization Movement,* AD 2000 Series (Birmingham, Ala.: New Hope, 1987), p. 45.

Tabernacle Presbyterian Church
Indianapolis, Indiana 46205